Dirt Roads and Bare Toes

J A Winstead

Text copyright © 2017 J A Winstead
All Rights Reserved

Dedication

I told my wife about some of my and my family's adventures while growing up in Nash County, North Carolina, and she suggested the next book I write should be about those stories. She thought the stories that I told her were both funny and interesting. So, because it was her idea, I dedicate this book to my loving wife Tammy.

J A Winstead

Introduction

When times were tough, the lessons learned from childhood to adulthood made you appreciate what life had to offer even in the smallest of ways. Most important, the resilience and endurance of the family bond along with the legacy of the simple but wonderful and delightfully curious by-gone days.

Dirt Roads and Bare Toes embraces a collection of heartfelt stories that have been stored in my mind for over seventy years, along with some contributed from my brothers and sisters as well. Follow along the journey of the strains and struggles while growing up, children of share-croppers, in Nash County, North Carolina. From the first word to the last, I hope these stories take you back to a simpler era and makes you long for more

Table of Contents

Dirt Roads and Bare Toes
A Day in The Days
Time to Go
Baby Boom
RC Cola
Something Rare
Guardian Angels
Stagecoach
Cheap Haircuts
Ghost on The Back Porch
Ghost Whisperer
Buster Brown Shoes
She Was a Lady
Mr. Buck and Bass Brothers
Stinging Worms
Hanging Out
The Dark Hole
She Got My Goat
Never Ever Run
William Don't Tell
The Great Train Ride
I Nailed It
We Were Flying
Whoops I Missed
My Brother Cecil And John Wayne
A Bomb?

Hit and Run
In the Wind
She's Funny You Know
One Footnote, Filed
Cigar Sick
Bottoms Up
Forgotten in Cotton
Early Bird Gets the Worm
A Rattle for My Baby Brother
Neighbor Nuisances
Going to Get My Shotgun
Parachute Drop
I Found My Thrill on Taylor's Hill
My Beautiful Corn Destroyed
Moms Are Smarter Than You Think
Nobody but Grandma
A Snowman?
In the Mood
My First Time
A Mighty Snore
Plant A Garden and They Will Come
Can We Ride the Horse?
A Bouquet for Their Mom
Ghost Bicycle
...And So, I Did
My First Arrest
Just Plain Stubborn

Dirt Roads and Bare Toes

There comes a time in everyone's life when they look back at where they came from and wonder if things would have been better by having more money, less money, a larger family or a smaller one. I don't know how many would like for their lives to have been different, but I'm pretty satisfied at the way my life developed.

For the most part, I was a happy kid with a great mom, dad, and seven siblings that lived very modestly in a very small house in Momeyer, North Carolina. I never knew how poor we were while growing up. I knew there were some that had more than us, but that didn't make me feel poor. In those days, no matter your wealth, people treated you with respect. When I played cowboys with the wealthier neighborhood kids, they had the double holsters and nice shiny pistols and I had a stick that was somewhat in the shape of a pistol. I never felt discriminated against because I didn't have a pretty blue bicycle or a Red Ryder BB gun. No, I think I felt as much a part of the neighborhood as anyone.

I was born in 1943, about a mile outside a small town called Spring Hope, North Carolina and about four miles from an even smaller community called, Momeyer. I don't know how old I was when we moved to Momeyer, but I was very young.

The house I was born in, in Spring Hope, Nash County, North Carolina. The house was torn down several years ago.

(Photo by Jimmy Winstead ©2017

I was one of ten children born to Raymond and Minnie Winstead. One of my brothers, Pete, who was the oldest of the siblings, died before I was born. Pete lived until the age of ten and died from eating green peanuts that poisoned him. Another brother, Hugh, died as a newborn baby and was born about seven or eight years after me. My brothers and sisters that I grew up with are, Richard, Floyd, Cecil, Barbara, Frances, Don and Terry.

My family; (left to right) back row: Richard, Floyd, Minnie (Mother), me (Jimmy), Don; middle row: Raymond (Daddy), Barbara, Cecil, Frances; front row: Terry.

(Photo Courtesy of Winstead Family ©2017)

    Writing this book brought back many memories of my childhood, and I thought it would be fun to go down memory lane and take you along, while I tell of some of the adventures that I experienced growing up. These are some of the stories of my father, mother, brothers, sisters, me and a few others.

A Day in the Days

Early in the mornings, say around sunrise, my mother would wake us up and tell us to get ready for breakfast. That aroma of freshly baked buttermilk biscuits, just cooked country ham and the smell of coffee brewing was like a powerful magnet that dragged you uncontrollably to the kitchen.

A platter that sat in the middle of the table would be piled high with beautiful, golden brown biscuits and next to that would be another plate with fresh country ham. Mother always made a bowl of red-eye gravy along with scrambled eggs and some hominy grits. To top it all off, there would be a jar of blackstrap molasses, Karo or King Syrup, patiently waiting for us to sop the biscuits in. The children were not allowed coffee, but instead there would be a pitcher of cold fresh milk with just a hint of cream on top that you would stir in before pouring. Our kitchen was large as it served as the dining room as well. The dining table was long with a bench on both sides that would seat four. There were eight children so a large table was a necessity. With a family of ten, it looked like a buffet when you walked in the kitchen.

After breakfast, I would go outside in the early morning while it was still cool and the warm sun was a reminder that the summer would soon be here and hot days were on their way. That was really not a big concern of mine at five or six years old, because at that age, working in the hot fields was not a job I had yet acquired. Mostly finding a way to entertain myself was the order of the day.

I can remember the sweet smell of honeysuckles and the earthy aroma of the freshly plowed fields. I would hear the buzz of bees around the wildflowers and the first sign of spring blossoms that filled the fruit trees. Spring was indeed one of my favorite seasons. On warm spring days, we shed our shoes and started the process of toughening up our feet for the summer. During the summer, you hardly ever wore shoes except to attend church. When my father would plow the land, the birds would follow him in the field to feast on earth worms that were exposed when the soil was turned inside out. I remember walking along the fence line that bordered the white sandy path and seeing a momma rabbit with her young kits in tow, scurrying for cover in the tall grass.

This was indeed a time of wonderment and a time that the rest of the world didn't matter, because I was in my own little world and it was good. My world was safe, time was slow, and you could actually lie on your back under a shade tree and not hear cars and trucks roaring up and down the road. You didn't see, or hear a plane rumbling across the sky. You didn't hear loud music, or someone cursing and arguing next door.

Thank God, I lived during those times and got to experience an era that you could leave your doors unlocked, day or night, whether you were at home or not. There were no locks on the barns or smokehouses and if you heard of a crime, it was usually in the big cities.

I remember our garden was large because this was how we made it through the winter months. Our garden consisted of sweet corn, okra, potatoes, tomatoes, cabbage, onions, beets, carrots, turnips, peppers, watermelons, cantaloupes, green beans, peas, cucumbers, strawberries and butter beans. I'm sure I've left something out, but by the time the fall months arrived, my mother had canned, along with the vegetables, fruits such as apples, pears, peaches, peach plums, figs, cherries, blackberries and huckleberries. Mother made pickles, preserves, jams and jellies. She would fill our pantry with a great assortment of canned fruits and vegetables that would be the pride of any housewife.

I know those days will never return, and only in memories can I re-live the peaceful warm feelings I had as a young boy. I never had to leave home to be somewhere I had never been. I could fly a fighter plane and shoot down the enemy, or be the captain of a ship, arrest bank robbers or be an army sergeant throwing grenades at the enemy. By the way, green pine cones made perfect grenades.

Wherever I wanted to be, or whatever I wanted to be was as simple as using my imagination to go there, and I spent many hours exercising that imagination as much as possible. So being a six-year-old son of a poor sharecropper never stopped me from having fun, or adventure. It was up to me, and I became a world traveler and explorer without ever leaving home.

My brothers, Floyd and Cecil and our sister, Frances and me.

(Photo Courtesy of Winstead Family ©2017)

Time to Go
(As told to me by Floyd E. Winstead)

My brother Floyd told me of an experience that he had, years before I was born, when our family lived in Rocky Mount. Floyd said the street they lived on was dirt like many of the streets at that time. The home that our family lived in did not have electricity and used oil lamps for lighting.

Floyd said that one early morning; he went to the front room in the house where he noticed a man sitting in a chair. The man was leaned back on the two back legs of the chair and against the wall, and that the man was reading a book. Floyd said that he stopped to look at the man but didn't know him, nor had he ever seen him before. The man never acknowledged Floyd being in the room. After staring at the man for a minute, he heard a horn that sounded like it was outside, and it also sounded like an old type horn with a honk-honk sound. After hearing the horn honk a couple of times, the man in the chair got up, closed his book and left.

Floyd says till this day, he still doesn't know who that man could have been, and nobody else knew and he thinks that the man was a ghost. The man looked as if he was waiting for a ride to go to work and when he heard the horn, he got up and left. Floyd said there was nothing really unusual about the man, that he was wearing a black waist coat and a black cap. He said that nobody lived there that looked like that person or went to work that time of morning. Creepy, huh?

Floyd Winstead

(Photo Courtesy of Winstead Family ©2017)

Baby-Boom

When I was just a tiny tot, probably around the time I was able to walk pretty good, I was next door at Mrs. Walston's house playing. As told to me later in my life by my mother, I was being watched by our neighbor's son, Joe, who was grown at the time. Anyway, as any little child would do, I was exploring the surroundings and being curious about things that I saw.

As time went by, I wanted to see what was under the porch. While under the porch, I found, on a floor joist, a small red box. I headed out from under the house, with the small red box in tow and back on the porch where I could see more clearly exactly what I had found. I tried to open the box but I just couldn't open it. I looked at the end of the porch and saw a hammer, it was big rubber hammer that people used back in those days to remove or to put a tire on a rim. I went and picked the hammer up walked back to where the little red box was at and sat down with the box between my legs. With both hands, I held the hammer above my head with all intentions of smacking the box with the hammer. Joe just happened to see me at that moment and called out to me, "Hold on there son, don't hit that box, let me see it first!" Mother said that I looked at Joe and lowered the hammer. Well thank God, I listened to him because it was a full box of dynamite caps.

Thanks Joe, you probably saved my life.

Mrs. Walston's house in Momeyer. The porch that the dynamite caps were under, collapsed many years ago and was torn down. We lived in the small, white house next door.

(Photo by Jimmy Winstead ©2017)

RC Cola

Once a month, or less, when I was a child did I ever get a soft drink. About the only way you could get a soft drink was if you worked on someone's farm and when you got paid, you were allowed to purchase some nonsense item that you didn't need such as, a five-cent cake, a soft drink, or five cents worth of candy. Otherwise, you were to save your money for school clothes and shoes.

One lucky morning, before I reached the age of working for my keep, I stepped out of the house into that wondrous world of curiosity and it was then I noticed something different at the edge of the road, across from the little store next door. I wondered out across our yard to get a better look. I saw a man sitting in a chair beside a multi-colored box. Well, that was something that had to be checked out. I sauntered along the side of the road until I had reached the man and the box. "Hello young man", the man said to me. "Would you like to have a RC Cola?"

Who are you kidding, I thought. "Yes Sir", I said, "I sure would!" The man smiled and reached into the cooler which was full of RC Colas and ice, retrieving a tall cold wonderful bottle of refreshing RC Cola. He popped the cap off and handed it to me. The only requirement of getting a free soft drink was to return the bottle when I finished and I promised that I would return with the empty. I thanked him and left to go back home sipping the sweet nectar from the bottle as I looked for a shady spot to enjoy my new-found pleasure. I don't think it took me too long to finish that one off. I went back to return the bottle as I had promised, and was greeted by the man again as he asked me if I liked the RC Cola. I told him that it was very good and that I liked it a lot. He asked me if I wanted another and I said, "Sure, thanks Mister!", and I was off with another one.

I'm not sure how much I weighed or exactly how tall I was, but I'm sure that on that day I made several trips down to that RC Cola box. I am pretty sure that a grown man would have had trouble drinking the amount of RC Cola's that I did on that day.

I know that it was a promotional thing for RC Cola, but it was an emotional thing for me, oh, and a lot of getting out of bed to go tinkle that night.

Tom Deans store in Momeyer. The RC Cola man had set up in the grass area across the street from Mr. Deans' store. Mr. Deans' store is no longer there.

(Photo Courtesy of Winstead Family ©2017)

Something Rare

Somewhere around the time when I was four years old I, like so many children in those days, wore a lot of hand-me-downs. Unfortunately, my older siblings that were closer to my age were girls. Therefore, that meant that either I wore some cute little skirts or flowered dresses or I had to look in other places for obtaining some boy clothes.

There was a boy in the neighborhood that was two or three years older than me. His family was wealthy compared to ours, and there were only two kids in their family unlike the eight kids in mine. I remember my mom took me to see this young boy's mom where apparently, an arrangement was made to pick up some used clothes that her son had out-grown. The boy always wore the best clothes and shoes, and he was a mama's boy, not that there's anything was wrong with that. I mean he was the younger of the two and the only boy. His sister was quite a bit older so that's why I referred to him as a mama's boy. The whole family was very nice and I knew them all until they passed away.

I watched as the lady took the clothes from the closet and handed them to my mother. My mother would look them over, hold them up next to me and say, "I think this will be just fine," or "I don't think he will be able to wear this." I had no say in the matter, so I just stood there and waited for this shopping spree to end.

As we gathered the clothes, which by the way was an arm full for both my mom and me, a man that worked for the family asked me as we were leaving, "Hey boy, what you going to do with all them clothes?" I told him that I was going to rare them! He laughed and said, "You're going to rare them?"

I said, "Yes sir." Ok, I was four years old and wear or rare didn't make a difference to me. For the rest of that man's life, whenever he saw me and even after I was grown, he called me Rare.

My brother, Richard, me and Daddy in a field of tobacco.

(Photo Courtesy of Winstead Family ©2017)

Guardian Angels

I truly believe that we all have guardian angels that watch over us, especially when we are children. There is no way I would be here without divine intervention. I remember as children we would go bare-footed all summer, running through the woods and weeds, the snake infested creek banks and never once getting bit by a snake, or ripping our feet open on sharp rocks or sticks.

One day when I was about four years old, my older brothers and sisters were in the front yard playing ball. I was just a spectator then since I was too young to join the team. I remember how they seemed to be having a really good time and I was a little jealous I couldn't play with them. One would hit the ball while the others would chase it and throw it back. On this one occasion, the ball came close to me and rolled into the road. I was excited that at last I had a chance to get my hands on that ball. I ran after it as hard as my little legs would take me, right out in front of a car. The car slammed on brakes but not before it had hit me, knocking me down and had rolled over top of me. A woman was driving the car, and she ran around to where I was sprawled out under the car like a mechanic. She was terrified, but I was as calm as could be. I guess I was too young to understand the danger and consequences of being ran over by an automobile. I don't think it scared me at all. I was not in the least hurt, so I didn't see where it was a big deal. Apparently, the lady saw me in time to brake the car and slow it down so by the time it hit me, it was really just a bump.

That little episode is just one of many times my guardian angel was watching after me when I was young, but, I believe my guardian angel has been with me all my life.

Our family; (left to right) back row: Richard, Mother (Minnie); middle row: Don (in Daddy's arms), Daddy (Raymond), Floyd; front row: Cecil, Frances, Barbara and me.

(Photo Courtesy of Winstead Family ©2017)

Stagecoach

Between 1948 and say 1958, my sister Frances and I would find hours of entertainment from using our imagination. I remember how she would play cowboy with me as long as she could be Roy Rogers, the King of the Cowboys. I on the other hand had to be next best, which according to her, was Gene Autry. She had her faithful steed, Trigger and I had mine, Champ. We spent hours rounding up rustlers and bank robbers.

Near our home and down in the cow pasture, was an old truck cab, with faded-out green paint and rust. The front of the truck was missing and it had no rear end, but what it did have was a close resemblance to that of a stagecoach. The old truck had doors, windows and a seat inside for passengers. We would sit on top of the truck with our feet placed on what was left of the front of the truck.

Sometimes getting to the stagecoach was a challenge. We had to crawl under the fence that was around the pasture and sneak by a big red bull. That bull was not a pet, nor one to play with. He ran our father up a pear tree, and kept him hostage there for about an hour.

Anyway, after avoiding the bull and finding safety on our stagecoach, we were transporting gold and passengers to their destination, and Black Bart and his gang won't about to stop us. We had shootouts with the worst of them, but we always delivered the goods. Sometimes one of us would get wounded, but nothing serious enough to stop our cause. I think we probably had the advantage over the bad guys because it was our imagination and our story, and we could play it out anyway we wanted to, plus I think each of our pistols held a thousand bullets, for I never remember reloading.

I have a lot of fond memories of cowboys and Indians, being a soldier, a pilot, even a bootlegger or convict. We were many characters in our childhood, but most of all, we were brothers and sisters in true life. We've always shown our love for each other, and have a lot of memories that we share, good and bad. We always have and had each other's back, and that's not pretend.

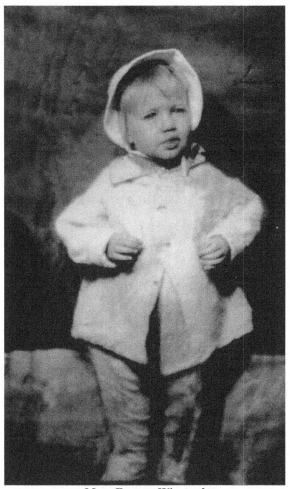

Mary Frances Winstead

(Photo Courtesy of Winstead Family ©2017)

Cheap Haircuts

While living in Momeyer I would go get a haircut at Tom Deans' barber shop, which was a tiny building in the parking lot, beside Bass Brothers store. Mr. Deans had two places of business, his store, which was close to where we lived and the barber shop. The barber shop was a very small building that was just big enough for a barber chair.

I seemed to never have any money but somehow managed to get whatever I needed or thought I needed. More than once I would make a trade with Mr. Deans for a haircut. I remember taking him some eggs and another time it was tomatoes. Whatever I could find, would be a fair trade for a haircut. I'm not so sure Mr. Deans felt the same way but he was very nice and always acted as if what I brought to him was exactly what he wanted or needed. One day I felt as if I needed to get a haircut, so off I went looking for something to trade.

I went up to Mr. Charlie Matthews' house seeking to find something for my trade deal. Under a big oak tree, I saw Norman Richardson. I'm not sure if Mr. Richardson worked for Mr. Matthews or was just a friend but in any case, we started talking and I told him I needed something to trade Mr. Deans for a haircut. He said that he didn't have anything, but there were a lot of acorns lying around under that big oak tree and Mr. Tom just might like to have a bag of them. I remember Mr. Richardson got me a paper sack and I filled it with acorns. I carried my bag of acorns proudly to the barber shop where Mr. Deans was sitting in the barber chair reading a newspaper. "What did you bring me today?" he asked.

"I brought you a big bag of acorns." I said.

Mr. Deans sort of laughed and said, "Well son, I could use a bag of acorns, thank you. Now I suppose you could use a haircut."

I said, "I sure can." So out of the chair he went, and in the chair, I went. I don't ever remember paying cash money for a haircut at Mr. Tom Deans' Barber Shop.

Ghost on Our Back Porch

One night, around eight or nine o'clock, I had to go to the outhouse to tinkle. I was only about five or six and the outhouse was some ways from the house and it was dark so I decided to just go off the back porch. There was nothing behind our house but trees and no light on the porch, so no one would know but me that I was going to pee off the end of the porch.

Carefully, I inched toward the end of the porch so as not to fall off because there was a ditch, at least six to eight feet deep right at the end of our porch. As I looked down to check my distance from the edge, I stopped and then I looked up. There, even with me, and looking me in the eye was a man wearing a, sort of, square looking cap that was flat on top. He had on a white long sleeved shirt with a dark, or to me black, vest over his shirt. He had a thick gray mustache and eyebrows. He didn't seem threatening, in fact, he was a very pleasant and kind looking old gentleman. I was not frightened at all by his sudden presence. The man would have had to been at least eight feet tall to have looked me in the eye. He never said anything, but then he just faded into the darkness as quietly as he had appeared. At that point, I don't think I ever relieved myself, but just turned and went back inside and sat on the floor against the wall not mentioning what had happened to me to anyone.

I think the reason I didn't say anything at the time is because I was more confused than scared. We didn't have a television, so we never saw or heard of any ghost stories, and I don't think I was really sure at exactly what I saw. I didn't mention that experience to anyone until I was about twenty years old. I told my brother Don about it one day when we had gone back to the neighborhood to just look around and reminisce about the times back then.

Not too long after Don and I had discussed the house and the ghost, I was telling my oldest brother Richard about it. He said, "Well you know about the ghost cat that I saw in the same house, don't you?"

I said, "No, I didn't know anything about a ghost cat." So, then Richard told me the story.

It seems that one night when Richard was going out of the bedroom, he saw a white cat walk into the room where he was at. The thing is, the cat came from a door that was closed and then walked across the room and went into the other wall, like there was a door there previously. He said that he tried calling to the cat, but the cat acted as if he was not even there.

Ghost house still standing as of 2017, but is slowly being taken over by nature. This house is right beside Mrs. Walston's old house in Momeyer.

(Photo by Jimmy Winstead ©2017)

Ghost house porch in back has collapsed or was torn down. This would have been the angle where the man was facing me.

(Photo by Jimmy Winstead ©2017)

Ghost Whisperer
(As told to me by Barbara Ann Winstead Ball)

Many years ago, my eldest sister, Barbara told me of an experience she had in the same house that I had seen the man off of the back porch. She was a very young girl at the time and like me, the whole episode was more confusing than scary, and this is her story.

Barbara said that one night she got out of bed to go use the potty which was located in my dad and mom's bedroom. As she started through the living room, she saw a man sitting in a rocking chair reading a newspaper. She said that when she went by, she didn't recognize him but she still said hello to him. She said that the man completely ignored her and said nothing, so she continued on to our parents' bedroom. She went over to where my mother was sleeping and shook her awake. Barbara asked Mother who the person was in the living room sitting in the rocking chair. She said that Mother told her to go back to bed that she must be dreaming. Barbara said that on her way back to get in her bed, she stopped and rested her hand on the back of the rocking chair and leaned forward so she could see his face and whispered, "What is your name?" Still the man said nothing as if he couldn't see her or hear her, so she just shrugged her shoulders and went back to bed.

Barbara says to this day, she knows that what she saw was indeed a ghost.

Barbara Ann Winstead

(Photo Courtesy of Winstead Family ©2017)

Buster Brown Shoes

From the best of my recollection, the Buster Brown shoe incident happened about 1949 and I would have been about six years old. We lived about a quarter mile from Bass Brothers store in the Momeyer community. Now, Bass Brothers' carried everything from horse collars to bobby pins. One of the Bass brothers said that if they didn't have it in their store, you didn't need it anyway.

Well, one day I decided I needed some shoes, but of course I didn't have the money to buy them. Thinking long and hard, I thought I would get the deposits from some soft drink bottles and then buy my shoes. Back in those days, soft drink manufacturers would offer you money, called a deposit, if you returned the empty glass bottle. The manufacturers would then recycle the bottles by cleaning and refilling them.

I just happened to know of where there were a whole lot of empty bottles and I was going to cash in on them. I took a little, rusty toy wagon and pulled it down to the store. I went behind the store where there were several crates of empty drink bottles. I filled my wagon with all it would hold and pulled it back around to the front of the store. I went inside where an employee, Mr. Buck Edwards, asked me what he could do for me. Everybody in and around Momeyer knew each other and who's kids belonged to who. "I want some shoes Mr. Buck," I said, "I want some of them Buster Brown shoes", as I pointed at a picture of Buster Brown and his dog that hung on the wall near the shoes. Buster Brown shoes were very popular back then, a well-known name brand, with very colorful advertising posters. Advertising posters on the store walls is how they got your attention because there was no television.

"You got any money?" he asked. I told him that I had a lot of bottles outside and he could have them for the shoes. I remember him laughing and patted me on my head and saying, "Take those bottles back around there and put them *back* in the crates, then come back in here." I did like he told me and returned to the store shoe department where I found Mr. Buck looking at some shoes in a box. He told me to sit and hold my foot up while he measured and found the perfect fit and slipped a brand-new pair of Buster Brown shoes on my feet. When I went into that store, I was bare footed, but I left with a great pair of Buster Browns, and I am sure that would probably never happen these days. He knew where the bottles came from and didn't have to give me the shoes but he was a very nice man, not only that time or just to me, but to everyone all the time.

I don't think I knew it was wrong to take the bottles, I just knew you could get money or things from the store if you turned them in. I never thought it mattered where the bottles came from. Anyway, all the Bass brothers were nice people and employed nice people to work for them, and I'm glad that I got to know them.

(Photo Courtesy of Bass Bros. ©2017)

She Was a Lady

Another little story that involved Bass Brothers store happened when I was about six years old. Our family had a dog which was a white Eskimo Spitz and her name was Lady. Lady was as much a part of our family as any of us were.

Every so often when my dad, mother or just one of us kids went to Bass Brothers store, Lady was sure to follow. Not so much that Lady wanted to go for a walk or keep someone company, but she went to the store for ice cream. As soon as she entered the store she would make a beeline for the ice cream box. Lady would sit up and beg and sometimes she would bark to get the clerk's attention, whoever it might be. More often than not, the clerk would be Mr. Buck Edwards. Mr. Buck would smile and come over giving Lady a scratch behind her ears and then a cup of vanilla ice cream. When she finished the ice cream she would sit up again and then shake hands with Mr. Buck before leaving. I think Lady was the only dog allowed to enter the store.

Speaking of ice cream, I remember paying five cents for a cone of ice cream. When Mr. Buck made you a cone of ice cream, it was piled as high as he could get it without fear of it toppling over. You always got more than your money's worth. Thanks Mr. Buck, I miss those days.

Me and Lady

(Photo Courtesy of Winstead Family ©2017)

My brother, Don with Lady.

(Photo Courtesy of Winstead Family ©2017)

Mr. Buck and Bass Brothers
(As told by Mary Frances Winstead Morris)

Somewhere around 1948 or 49, I remember it was a hot sultry afternoon in Momeyer, when I was on my way home from school. There was only one week left of school before the summer will be mine. I have an uncontrollable urge to rip off my sweaty shoes and worn socks and scrunch my bare feet and toes in the white silky sand, but I know I had better wait till the late evening when the sand has cooled a bit.

I turned my attention to Bass Brothers General store and stepped up on those familiar creaky steps that led me to the crowded porch. A walkway led me through tall stacks of gleaming galvanized buckets, standing there like the armored knights of King Arthurs Court. There were wooden barrels, kegs of nails, screws and bolts, and a variety of goods used by the farmers. Farming was the biggest industry in and around Momeyer, and if you didn't have a farm, you more than likely worked for someone that did.

As I reached the screen door, my eyes were level with the Merita Bread sign door push with the bright word written in red cursive, "Merita" with green and yellow circles around it. Just about every store you went in, that was located in Nash County had a Merita, a Pepsi, or Dr. Pepper door push, and for those that don't know what a door push is, it's a metal sign with an advertisement on it that is put on the screen doors of stores so that when people push the door open, it prevents them from pushing the screen out of the door.

I stepped inside the store, and I was met with the aroma of fresh sawdust that was put on the floor to prevent dust in the air when people walked through. The smell of ripe apples and peaches captured my nostrils as I inhaled deeply to savor the moment. As I walked across the sawdust floor, my feet did a little slow dance.

Right in the middle of the store sat a large ice-cream box, tempting everyone that passed it on those hot and humid summer days. Then just to the left of me stood a large wooden showcase with a glass front to show off all the candy dreams of young boys and girls. But, on that day, my eyes were focused on one thing, the ice cream box. The image in my mind of a huge chocolate cone of ice cream was making my mouth water.

I didn't have a penny, or anything that even resembled money, but just the thought of that ice cream made me all cool and quivery inside. I could almost feel that cold mountain of chocolate ice cream on my tongue. When I returned to reality, ole tall, skinny Mr. Buck was looking down at me with his familiar grin and wanted to know if he could help me. I blurted out that I couldn't make up my mind. Embarrassed that I had no money, I sprinted off to the back of the store where I always stopped to get a refreshing drink of water from their water cooler. As I leaned over the cooler, and before my lips touched that cool stream of water, my eyes fixed on a small shiny, silver object on the corner of the cooler, it was a nickel, an honest to goodness American, Indian-head nickel. My guardian angel must have known how much my heart wanted Mr. Buck to reach way down in that big cardboard ice cream bucket and come up with the world's biggest scoop of chocolate ice cream that he could possibly plop on one ice cream cone. Mr. Buck was the only person to wait on you that understood the yearnings of children. He seemed to make sure that he was the one to wait on us when we came in the store so that we would be sure to get more than our money's worth. He knew how hard and how far in between it was that we got any money, so he wanted to make sure we enjoyed it whenever we had it.

My face was flushed with anxiety as I ran back down the aisle to the ice cream box. For some mysterious reason, Mr. Buck was still standing there. A big smile crossed his face and he asked me if I had made up my mind yet? All the while, he was holding an empty ice cream cone. How he knew that I would be back, is certainly a mystery to me. He knew I had no money when I ran off like I did, but yet, he waited for me to return. He also knew that chocolate was my favorite flavor, so he reached down deep into the chocolate and came up with a dollar's worth and plopped it on the cone. He pushed and pushed, until he was satisfied that I had gotten more than my nickel's worth. Holding the cone of ice cream out to me, and with a big smile on his face, he said, "That will be exactly one nickel please."

I was grinning from ear to ear as I took the cone and handed him the nickel. I said, "Thank you Mr. Buck," then I just floated out the back door and headed home.

Some things you forget when you are a child, and some things you want to forget. Things like that wonderful chocolate ice cream cone, Mr. Buck's gentle smile and the days I visited Bass Brothers store are days I don't want to forget. Such good memories.

Mary Frances Winstead

(Photo Courtesy of Winstead Family ©2017)

Stinging Worms!

When I was about six years old, I was down behind the house in the orchard and headed to the stables when I decided to get an apple for ole Betsy. Betsy was a small mule there on the farm. In Betsy's younger days, she was a logging mule and no matter what you hooked her up to, she wanted to pull it as fast as she could. She was a gentle mule and we could ride her anytime or place and she never tried to buck or throw any of us off her back. I liked ole Betsy a lot.

Anyway, I wanted to get an apple for her because she always enjoyed them so much. I looked up in the tree and saw a large red, juicy-looking apple almost at the top of the tree. Just so you know, earlier that day, one of my older brothers had pointed out some fuzzy worms on the trunk of a tree and told me they were stinging worms and not to touch them because they had a really bad sting. So, later on that day when I climbed the tree for the apple, I was watching where I placed my feet on the limbs instead of looking up to see that I was about to stick my head right into a big wasp nest the size of a basketball. Needless to say, they wrapped my little head up, and of course the first thing I thought of while I was being stung on every inch of my face was that they were stinging worms. I couldn't run so I just yelled out, "Stinging worms, thousands of them!"

My dad came to see what was going on and saw that I was trying to get away from the wasps, so he told my brother Floyd to go help me down. Floyd told my dad that he didn't want to go up there and be stung too. I couldn't stand it anymore so I just turned loose the branches and did a free fall. Fortunately, the good Lord was with me and some smaller branches slowed my fall and I think I landed on my feet.

My sister Frances led me to the house because both my eyes were swollen shut. My face and head was swollen so big, my dad said I couldn't put my head in a five-gallon bucket. Back then you didn't go to the hospital emergency room for stuff like that. Mother put wet snuff spittle on the areas affected to take the sting out, and it worked.

Hanging Out

When we were living on the Mathews farm, and I'm not sure how long we stayed there, because I think we moved at least every three years at the most. We were sort of like nomads, looking for greener pastures and traveling from farm to farm. A Ma and Pa Kettle family, dirt poor share croppers looking for a better life. But at my young age, life was wonderful and the time we spent on Mr. Mathew's farm are some of my most favorite memories from my childhood.

Now to tell you the truth, I have some unclear memories of things that happened when I was so young, but for the most part, I do remember things like my brother Cecil, sisters, Barbara, Frances and myself playing in the old hay barn. We were playing cowboys and bank robbers. My brother was the robber and my sisters and I were the posse. Well, after a shootout and a brief scuffle, we captured the bad guy and tied his hands and hauled him off to jail. After the trial, we decided that hanging him would be the appropriate punishment, so off to the gallows we went, time for him to pay for his life of crime.

Cecil was the oldest of the four, so as the plot moved ahead, he would instruct us on how things were to be done. He told us that when you go to hang a man, you tie his hands behind him. Then you stand him on a bale of hay, and put a rope around his neck, then throw the other end over the rafters and secure it to the wall. We very carefully followed all of his instructions. The last thing you would think a person in their right mind would tell someone to do while they have a noose around their neck is to push the bale of hay out from under them. What my brother Cecil was thinking, I don't know, but that's exactly what he told us to do. So, we pushed the bale of hay out leaving him dangling about two feet off the floor. His face turned red and he was mumbling something about killing us when he got down. So, we were not waiting around to find out what he would do.

We ran down out of the barn where we just happened to run into our mother. She said that we were to go to the house for supper, and then asked where Cecil was at. I think Frances or Barbara told her that he was hanging in the barn. Mother ran up the stairs of the barn to find Cecil with a blue face hanging by the neck. She instructed one of the girls to untie the rope as she held him up to relieve the tension. I can't remember much after that, but I don't think Cecil had any lingering injuries from that particular day, but probably added an inch to his height. Oh, and by the way, he didn't try to kill us for hanging him.

My brother, Cecil, and sister, Barbara.

(Photo Courtesy of Winstead Family ©2017

The Dark Hole

My sister Frances reminded me of the time she wanted me to help build her a playhouse when we were living in Momeyer. Back then everyone knew everyone and their children, even their pets most of the time, but sometimes that would not keep you safe from dangers around the neighborhood.

There was a path that ran by our house and continued behind the house while passing by the hay barn and stables. Follow the path just a little further along and it came to a very large old dilapidated cotton gin. I don't know how many years it had been shut down, but it must have been quite a few. Mind you, we were very young, Frances was probably around eight and I was about six, and the cotton gin was off limits to us. The cotton gin was a very intriguing place, a wonderland of mystery and adventure. There were machines like we had never seen before, and it was a castle or haunted house or whatever a young imagination wanted it to be.

The fact remains that old cotton gin was dangerous and we were warned to stay out of it. But just like most kids, we thought we knew how to take care of ourselves, and nobody would be the wiser if we went in there to play.

One day Frances asked me if I would help her get a wooden board that was on the second floor of the cotton gin. The board was about three feet by three feet square, just right for a table top to go on a table in her playhouse. I agreed to help her, so off we went to collect the board. Frances got on one side of the board and me the other. We lifted the board with little effort and I started to walk backwards and as I took a step or to back, Frances of course took a couple of steps forward, and when she did, she fell into a hole that the board was covering. Luckily, her falling caused us to drop the board and she fell with both her arms over the board, stopping her from falling all the way through. I reached out and took her by her hands and pulled her back up. When we looked down that dark hole we could see on the bottom floor a couple of large rollers that looked like those round hair brushes, except instead of plastic bristles, they were long sharp steel spikes about a foot long.

Later on, I found out that the large spiked rollers were used to comb out the cotton seeds from the cotton. That was a scary experience, but I'm sure in the next hour we were probably back in there looking something else to go in her playhouse.

Frances just told me recently that we must have had a very watchful guardian angel back then because we were always doing something, and a lot of the time it was dangerous. Now that we look back at it, it was just another day in the life of Frances and Jimmy with a need to explore our own little world that would challenge our ingenuity and open up new ideas that would feed our hunger for adventure.

She Got My Goat

When I was around seven years old and living in Momeyer, a dirt road separated our house from a cow pasture that had both cows and goats in it. One day I was out in the front yard playing when I saw a large white goat with huge horns, jump right over a low spot in the fence where the wire was sagging a bit. I was not afraid of the goat so I continued playing and sort of forgot about him.

After a few minutes had passed, I happened to glance out the corner of my eye to see this large white goat with huge horns. I could tell by the way he was pawing the ground and shaking his head that this was not a friendly gesture! I quickly measured with my eyes the distance I had to run to get to the house, or to the nearest tree. My quick calculations led me to plan A, which was the house. I didn't take time to weigh the difference, so I took off running as fast as my little skinny legs could take me, looking back only once to see if the goat had gained any ground on me. Sure enough, he was gaining on me as I reached our front porch. Being summer, the screen door was the only door I had to open to reach safety. I flung the door open and was inside the house when right behind me, I heard the goat crash right through the screen door. I ran to the stairs with the goat right on my heels. Up the stairs we went when I heard my mother yelling at me for bringing a goat in the house. I yelled back down to her that the goat had chased me into the house.

Mother was afraid of little or nothing and the idea of a goat in the house was bad news for the goat. Mom grabbed her trusty broom and commenced to bang that goat over his head.

The goat I think was more amused at the activity than hurt. I told my mother that she was hitting the wrong end of that goat. She started swatting his behind with the handle of that broom and that got his attention. That goat turned around and bolted out the door the way he came in.

There were several of those goats in that pasture, but that particular one I knew when I saw him. I think he remembered me too as he always shook his head when he saw me and would stick his tongue out at me when I passed by.

Never Ever Run

Somewhere around the age of seven, my mother and dad left my oldest sister, Barbara, in charge of the younger kids while mom and dad trekked off to town to buy goods that we didn't grow or make on the farm.

If you were born before the sixties, you probably remember that there were two rooms in the house or at least in our house, that you didn't go in unless your parents were there to give their permission. Those two off-limit rooms were my parent's bedroom and the living room.

Your parents just knew that if you were given the chance, you would snoop around in their bedroom and find out the mystery of adulthood. The reason you didn't go into the living room is because that's where only company was allowed to go. The best couch, chairs, tables and lamps were there and we were not allowed to sit on them or to even visit them. Those two rooms were strictly off limits.

On that particular day while my parents were away, I decided to find out the secrets that lurked behind my parent's bedroom door. I was somewhat disappointed when I entered the room that it was just a simple room with a bed and a dresser and vanity. But then I thought, there must be more, so I began to do a little snooping around through the vanity when I came across a pretty blue and white box. I retrieved the box from the drawer and opened it to find some fancy stationary and a fountain pen. Well, you can't just look at something like that, you have to try it out. So, I took a sheet of that pretty light blue paper with that fancy border around it and placed it on the top of the vanity. There were white lace doilies atop the vanity to which I was so careful to move to the side. I took the fountain pen and attempted to draw a line across the paper, but soon realized the pen was empty of ink. I searched the drawer to find a full bottle of Scripto, jet black ink in the back of the drawer. I was excited to fill the pen the way I had seen my mother do, so I very carefully opened the bottle of ink and eased the pen into the ink. I pulled down the little lever on the side and my little finger slipped off and hooked the side of the bottle turning the bottle of ink over, and I mean all over, the vanity and those pretty white lacy doilies. The ink continued to pour down into the open drawer all over the rest of the stationary.

Fear will not describe what I was feeling at that moment. All I could think to do was to go get my sister Barbara and hope she could fix the mess I made before my mother returned. As soon as she saw what I had done, she started crying and said Mother is going to kill us. That made me think, why would she be in trouble when it was me that made the mess? Barbara was quick to inform me that she was left in charge of the younger kids, which made her responsible. I felt bad that I may have gotten Barbara in trouble over my bumbling blunder, but what was done, was done.

Barbara and Frances.

(Photo Courtesy of Winstead Family ©2017)

Now the agony of waiting, and wondering what the punishment would be for ruining my mother's vanity, her lacy white doilies, a box of her special stationary and a full bottle of ink and not to mention the fact that I was not allowed in that room in the first place.

After adding all these things up and the severity of my crime, only death could be worse the way I figured it.

Now the long wait before the execution, and hoping Mom had a good day and was in a good and forgiving mood. But in reality, I knew that was just wishful thinking. All the sins of being too nosey were coming down on me all at one time, and the fact that the executioner was my mother had no bearings on the situation what so ever, rules are rules.

Later that evening, I heard a car drive up to the house. This is it, life as I know it now, will change in a matter of minutes. This beautiful woman, this wonderful mother that has nourished and loved me all my young life is about to transform into a demon, or at least that's what I was thinking.

As Mother entered the house, Barbara met her and in a whimpering voice informed her of the catastrophic irreversible mess that I had made in Mom and Dad's bedroom. Without a word, Mom went out and broke off a switch (a limb or branch from a bush or tree for punishing a child, or better yet, a whipping tree) to carry out the execution with. I knew what was in store for me when she returned. Now I hear that dreaded call, "Jimmy, come here now!" I could feel a cold chill run down my spine as I walked toward her. A grimaced look, I'm sure, was on my face and I don't think I can describe the look on my mother's face except it was not a happy one.

"Come here boy, didn't I tell you not to play in our bedroom? Well, you did it this time and you are going to pay for it," she said. Again, she demanded that I go to her. My brain was telling me not to disobey her command, but my feet were telling me don't be stupid, run instead of getting your tail torn up by a very angry woman. My feet in this particular case won the conversation and I turned and ran. Oh, what mistakes we make as a child!

My mother yelled at me and said, "Boy, don't you run from me, it's going to be twice as bad if you don't come back here right now." My little ole feet just kept on running until I was out of sight and hearing distance. I didn't go all that far, just around the house and then under it where she couldn't reach me. I don't know what might have been under the house, but nothing was as scary as what was waiting for me on the outside. In a few minutes, she left and I heard her when she went back inside the house.

Now it was a waiting game for me, wondering what I was going to do next. I was sure that my mother was angry at me and how long it would take her to cool off was anybody's guess. So, there I was, under a dark dusty spider infested house and probably a few snakes and other creepy crawlers just waiting to crawl down my collar.

After about two hours, my mom came to the door and in a very pleasant voice called all of her dear little children by name; mine included, and told us to come inside for supper. At that moment, I had a revelation, I thought that my mom had cooled off and I could go in and of course be very polite and helpful and everything would be forgotten and forgiven. I tried being invisible while we had our meal, not to bring any attention to myself. My mom told my sister, Frances, to wash the dishes when we were through with supper and right away I asked Mom if she wanted me to dry the dishes and put them away as I was hoping to win a reprieve for my actions. "Yes," she said, "then get washed up and get ready for bed." Music to my ears! I was home free, safe from the gallows and without a scratch.

Pretty soon I was in my little tighty whities and slipping between those soft white sheets. A string from a light that hung in the middle of the celling was tied to the headboard of the bed so I could turn the light on or off without getting out of bed. I reached up pulled the string and complete darkness fell over me. In less than ten seconds, the light was switched on, and there stood my mother with that long buggy whip looking switch. If ever there was a time that the words, 'oh no', were appropriate, that was the time.

First of all, she pulled the sheet back exposing my little naked back and legs. Then she told me how many times I had been warned not to do things I had been told not to do. Then she commenced to ruin my night by whipping me good fashion. She said, "I hope this has taught you not to mess with things you've been told not to mess with." She then turned and turned the light off and left the room closing the door behind her. In less than two seconds the door opened again and the light was switched back on, and there stood my mother with what was left of the switch. "Now," she said, "this is for running from me today." Again, she put a whipping on me and said, "That's what you get when you run, one whipping for what you did and one for running."

Needless to say, I never ran again.

This was my mother's vanity. The ink stain is still visible in the top right drawer. My mother used to stand Frances on the little shelf in-between the drawers to dress her and to brush her hair when she was little.

(Photo Courtesy of Tammy Winstead ©2017)

William Don't Tell

My older brother Cecil was always coming up with a game or a new adventure for us to try and this particular day was no different.

Cecil suggested that we make some bows and arrows. His idea sounded good to me and my little brother Don just tagged along with us because Cecil was supposed to be watching him. Cecil suggested that we go and get some reeds to make our arrows. So off we went, excited about doing something besides being bored to death doing nothing. So now, we have gotten to the reeds and my brother cuts and strips them of their leaves. Holding them up to his eye and checking to make sure they were straight. Carefully he measured them to make sure they were all the same length.

Now, to make a bow, Cecil took a limb from a young sapling and tested its flexibility. He then measured it and cut it to size. Then he took some baling twine and affixed it to one end of the bow, put his knee in the middle of the limb, and bent it into a bow while he attached the twine to the other end.

Now it was time to turn the reeds into arrows, so the first thing was to attach feathers on the end to make it fly straight and true. Having a lot of chickens on our farm made finding feathers easy. For the arrowhead, Cecil went the shop and found some finishing nails, and inserted them in the other end of the reeds and then wrapped the end with string to help hold the nails in place.

Don and I looked on with great interest, hoping that we might get a chance to shoot that wonderful bow our big brother had constructed. At first, Cecil was reluctant to give us a turn, but finally let us give it a try.

After about thirty minutes of shooting a tree or the barn, Cecil decided that he had become quiet the archer, and need a more challenging target. He looked around and then fixed his eyes on our little brother Don, who was wearing a straw-hat. He said that he would rather have an apple, but the straw hat would do just as well. So, Cecil got Don to stand beside a tree and turned him to his side and told him to stand still.

Cecil walked off a few paces, took aim and let the arrow fly. The arrow found its mark striking the hat straight into its side, oh, and also straight into our little brother's head. Thank God, the bow was not very powerful, but it still stuck into Don's head. Cecil was frantic, not that he shot his little brother in the head with an arrow, but that mother would get his britches really good for doing such a dumb and dangerous thing to him instead of watching over him and protecting him.

After calming Don down and cleaning his head of blood, Cecil said, "Don't tell mother, she will be mad and punish us all if she finds out that we were shooting arrows at each other." I don't think mother ever knew about our little secret and I'm sure Don never forgot.

A few Winstead kids; (left to right) back row: Barbara, Frances, Cecil; front row: Me and Don.

(Photo Courtesy of Winstead Family ©2017)

The Great Train Ride

We lived just a short walk from the train tracks in Momeyer and my younger brother Don and I loved to watch the train go by. The train had a big old steam engine I think, and it would rumble and shake the ground beneath our feet when it came by, but was exciting and a little scary being around such a powerful machine. Don and I always talked about riding that train one day. The engineer would always blow the whistle as he came by and would throw us some candy, a nickel cake or sometimes bubblegum. We really looked forward to seeing that train and seldom missed seeing it every day as it came by. I never learned the engineer's name, but I wished I had because anyone that threw out candy on a daily basis had to be a very nice man.

One day Don and I were walking down by the tracks when we saw six or seven train cars just sitting there and no one around. It was more than we could resist. I helped Don in the car with the door that was open and I went right in behind him. For about two hours we pretended to be a couple of hobos that had jumped the train and headed for places unknown. The next day the cars were still there so we jumped aboard again for another adventurous day on the rails. After about twenty minutes of entertaining our wild imaginations, we heard the train coming down the tracks. We hid in the car so as not to be detected, so we would not have to get out. Very quietly we waited to see if the train was going to leave, but instead it backed up to the cars we were in, hooked to them and then started moving down the tracks. I looked at Don and he just shrugged his shoulders as to say, 'I don't know what to do'.

I was a little scared, but I told him that this was our chance to ride the train, "So let's do it". I could walk faster than the train was moving, but we were still riding the train. In less than three minutes, the train stopped with a jolt, almost throwing us to the front of the car we were in. We then waited for the train to move again but it didn't, or at least the car we were in didn't. After a minute or two we heard the train chugging on down the line and without us. Apparently, they were shuffling some cars around and at the time we didn't realize that the cars we were in were sitting on a side track. Our great train ride went the distance of maybe fifty yards, what a bummer!

Train tracks in Momeyer, scene of *The Great Train Ride*.

(Photo Courtesy of Jimmy Winstead ©2017)

I Nailed It

When I was about eight years old, one day I jumped off the top of the chicken house and my right foot found a rusty nail that was in a board on the ground. The nail was about two and a half inches, and every bit of the nail was in my foot. I sat down and tried to pull on the board that held the nail but couldn't pull the nail free of my foot. Holding the board in my right hand while I hopped on the other foot, I made it to our backdoor steps where I called out to my mother to come and help me. Mother came out and summed up the situation and what to do. She got in front of me and grasped the board and gave it a quick jerk and out came the nail.

Mother poured kerosene over the wound and then wrapped it with a piece of a brown paper bag and then wrapped over the brown paper some white material. She said that the kerosene would take the soreness out and the paper bag would not let the kerosene build up heat and blister my foot. I'm not sure that was the correct way to give first aid to that sort of wound, but it sure worked. The next day I was running around and my foot was not sore at all.

We Were Flying

In the fall of the year we harvested our corn. It seemed to always be cold in early morning when we went to the field. My older brother, Cecil, would drive the tractor and my sisters, Barbara and Frances, and myself would ride on the trailer behind the tractor. When we got to the field, the tractor and trailer would be parked out away from the field until the corn had been pulled and thrown into a pile between the rows. Each of us would take a row of corn and pull it and throw it into a single pile. Sometimes an ear of corn was so tough to pull off the stalk, you would have to twist and twist until it finally broke free. At the end of the day your hands would be sore and rough. By the time we had reached the end of the field, there were several piles of corn from one end to the other and before we went back to the house the corn had to be loaded on the trailer. So now Cecil would drive the tractor alongside the piles of corn while we picked it up and threw it on the trailer. After all the corn had been picked up we were ready to head back to the house to unload it into the corn crib.

Barbara, Frances and I were sitting atop the load of corn while Cecil was driving the tractor. He picked up speed more and more and we were laughing and enjoying the fast ride down a white sandy path. Our day of labor was almost over but then without any warning the trailer became disconnected from the hitch on the tractor and the tongue of the trailer went to the ground and stuck. The momentum of the trailer caused the rear of the trailer to lift, and it sent the three of us flying, along with a whole load of corn. Cecil didn't even know he had lost us until he had gone another hundred yards. He turned the tractor around and went back to where we were submerged in a cloud of dust, sand and corn. Fortunately, no one was injured. The worst part of it all was that we had to pick all that dang corn up again!

We were sworn to secrecy by Cecil not to mention the three flying kids and the trailer of corn mishap.

After a day of pulling, throwing and picking up corn, your hands were red and chafed so we would rub Corn Huskers Lotion on our hands and that seemed to make them feel a little better. I tell you this, just in case you have to pull corn one day.

Roy Cecil Winstead

(Photo Courtesy of Winstead Family ©2017)

Whoops, I Missed

When I was around nine years old, my eldest brother, Richard, came home from the army. He served and fought in Korea. I'm sure there were things that bothered him and he probably suffered from post-traumatic stress disorder and to what degree, I don't know. However, it turns out that the rest of the family at times would catch the fallout from it.

Richard Winstead

(Photo Courtesy of Winstead Family ©2017)

One day, I was sitting on our front porch steps when Richard came out of the house upset about something. On his way down the steps he smacked me behind my head and told me to get out of the way. Well I knew I was not in his way because before I could move, he passed on by. Then he turned as if he had forgotten something and started back into the house. This time as he started by me and smacked me with his knee and told me to get out of his way. The next time, when he came back out, he did the same thing and smacked me even harder and I was too stubborn to move. I felt I was not blocking the steps and I was not going to move. I looked over by the porch post and saw an empty Pepsi Cola bottle. I stood up, grabbed that bottle and just like throwing a baseball, threw the bottle as hard as I could, trying to hit him in the back of his head. The bottle whizzed by his head and hit the windshield of his car, shattering the windshield.

Richard turned and I could see fire in his eyes and smoke coming out of his ears. I knew I was dead meat unless I could manage to get to Mother first. So, like a bullet, I was through the front door and yelling for mom. I found Mom in the kitchen just as Richard caught up to me yelling that he was going to kill me. Mother stepped between us and told him he was not to touch me, and that she wanted to know what was going on. I explained to her what happened and why I threw the bottle at him and not the car. Mother told Richard that he was lucky the windshield stopped the bottle rather than his head, but he deserved what he got for picking on his brother. She also warned him not to seek revenge on me later or he would have to deal with her.

Now be advised, you didn't want to be on the wrong side of Mother, I don't care how old you were, she was still Mother and she would put you in your place.

God bless her soul, she had a hard life, but she never wavered in being a sweet loving mother. I miss her!

Richard's car at the Pepsi Cola bottle incident. This was Boone's farm.

(Photo Courtesy of Winstead Family ©2017)

My Brother Cecil and John Wayne

My older brother Cecil was quiet the character and always had a funny story to tell or a game that he thought up for us to play. One day we went to a neighbor's house there in the community to play with a playmate of ours. This young boy always had the best in toys like, double holstered, pearl handled, silver pistols, with Roy Rogers, King of the Cowboy's gloves with the fringe cuffs, and a cowboy hat and boots. My brother and I had a stick! In some cases, the stick may resemble a pistol if your imagination was strong enough and you didn't look at it too long. I guess back then you had to use your imagination in order to survive poverty. We knew our parents couldn't afford to give us things that other kids may have, but they were able to teach us how to use our imagination, and do with what we had.

On this particular day, our playmate's cousin was visiting him, and no joke, his real name was John Wayne. We decided to play cowboys and robbers. Because of us having less than the cowboy's garb, my brother and I were the robbers.

We ran about being chased by the sheriff and his posse, across the Bad Lands and through the canyons until finally we had to stop and shoot it out. My brother and I found cover behind a large oak tree, whereas the sheriff and his deputy, John Wayne, were right out in the open. We exchanged gunfire for a few minutes when my brother Cecil exclaimed that he shot John Wayne, but John Wayne said that my brother missed because he ducked the bullet. John Wayne kept advancing on us, and no matter how many times my brother said that he shot John Wayne, Mr. Wayne said that my brother missed because he ducked the bullet. Well pretty soon John

Wayne was close enough to my brother, that my brother reached out and smacked John Wayne on his head with the stick (pistol) and said, "Did you duck that?" Needless to say, John Wayne went crying to his mommy, and we high tailed it back to our bunkhouse.

Cecil riding Betsy in Momeyer.

(Photo Courtesy of Winstead Family ©2017)

A Bomb?

Between 1950 and 1953, my oldest brother Richard, was fighting in the Korean War. My mother received letters from him telling us of things that were going on over there. My mother would always read the letters to us and I remember him saying things that were scary, like bombs bursting, and bullets flying and all the chaos that they had to endure.

I remember Richard's letters sometime would have mud stains and sometimes the ink would run where the letter got wet before he could send it. My mother kept all his letters, however I don't know what happened to them.

On a warm summer morning I was playing out in the yard, and like a cloud blocking the sun, a large shadow appeared. I looked up and to my surprise, there was a large metallic colored object, one like I had ever seen before, was looming just above the tree tops. Totally frightening my britches off, I ran inside to get my mother and told her that there was a big bomb right over our house. She didn't have any idea what I was talking about but went outside to investigate my claim. When she looked up, found it to be a dirigible and explained to me what it was. I was so relieved to see her smile as she watched the dirigible disappear over another stand of trees.

I guess since there was a war going on, and hearing about bombs and such, plus the fact that I had never seen a blimp or dirigible airship, my imagination led me to believe the worst was about to happen and we were about to be bombed.

As a side note, all five of my brothers, Richard, Floyd, Cecil, Don, Terry, including myself, served in the military and all six of us were proud to serve our country.

Richard Winstead while in the army.

(Photo Courtesy of the US Army ©2017)

Floyd Winstead while in the army.

(Photo Courtesy of the US Army ©2017)

Cecil Winstead while in the army.

(Photo Courtesy of Winstead Family ©2017)

Me in the army.

(Photo Courtesy of the US Army ©2017)

Don Winstead while in the army.

(Photo Courtesy of Winstead Family ©2017)

Terry Winstead while in the army.

(Photo Courtesy of the US Army ©2017

Hit and Run

At sometimes in everyone's life, I think you want to be a cowboy. Riding the range, robbing trains, or having a shootout with the bad guys. I know when I was just a little greenhorn myself, my imagination was as big as it gets. I could straddle a tobacco stick or broomstick and ride with the best of them. I was the sheriff, the marshal, or the bank robber that was hanged for his bad deeds.

On one particular sunny spring day, I was in the field with my older sister Barbara. I'm not even sure what the job at hand was, but apparently, I was not in the mood to do my part. So, I was in my own little world playing cowboy and throwing clods of dirt across the field making the dust fly like a bullet ricocheting off the ground like you see in the movies. That was fun for a while, but just not real enough. I mean, who just shoots at the ground?

So, I looked around and saw Barbara slaving away at her chores. Now that could very well be a cattle rustler I was seeing out there across the prairie. I loaded up the old Winchester and commenced to fire away, causing a puff of dust to fly pretty close to my sister. My sister warned me several times to stop throwing those clods of dirt towards her, that I may hit her. Well what kind of sheriff would I be if the crook told me to stop and I did? Sometimes a shot came very close to her and she would give me that, 'keep on until you hit me and it going to get your britches look'.

If you think for a minute that she was a pushover because she was a girl, you would be very wrong. My sister had a pretty face, but she also had a mean right hook.

Well it was bound to happen, this clod of dirt struck Barbara on her shoulder, and I remember her throwing down the hoe she was using, thank goodness, and took off after me. I felt an urgent urge to flee while there was still life in me. I looked over my shoulder and I could see her coming across that field with a plume of dust behind her like a herd of wild horses running across the plains of Wyoming. She was gaining on me fast and I knew what was instore when she caught me. As she finally caught up with me and pushed me in the back causing me to fall forward and allowing my chin to plow a new row in the field. Barbara flipped me over on my back and pinned my shoulders to the ground. Staring down at me with sweat dripping off her nose and on to my face. Her face was red and she was clinching her tongue between her teeth. I closed my eyes not wanting to see what was coming next. But then, she just scolded me and told me that I better not do that again, or I wouldn't be that lucky.

I'm not saying this just because she let me off with a warning, but Barbara has always treated me good and all my life let me know how much she loves me. Love you Bob. That's what I called her when I was growing up, Bob.

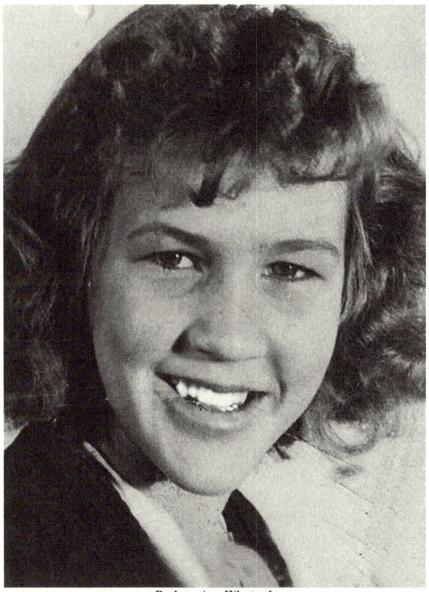
Barbara Ann Winstead

(Photo Courtesy of Winstead Family ©2017)

In the Wind

Somewhere around the age of ten years old, I remember our family taking a trip to the beach. As usual, if we went anywhere, it was an adventure. Are you kidding, we are going to the beach! I can't remember all that clearly, but I think we were going on our cousin's truck. I think my father and cousin, and maybe one more were riding in the cab of the truck, and the rest of the clan was in the back. The truck had a canvas top and sides on it which helped to keep the hot sun from bearing down on us. I'm sure back then we were probably roaring down the road at a top speed of at least forty-five mph. My mom sat in the back against the cab where she could keep an eye on the bunch. Mother had a chair that she sat in, and we probably looked like the Clampetts from the Beverly Hillbillies show on our way to Hollywood.

You see, with the size family we had, there was not enough room for the whole family to get into one car, so that's why we were in that truck. I think counting my cousin, there was ten of us all together.

On our way there, we didn't stop for fast food, as there was hardly a place back then that had fast food. No, we always carried what we were going to eat, there was no way my dad could afford to feed that crowd in a restaurant. It was bologna sandwiches and banana sandwiches and maybe a ham biscuit or two. Never mind that the temperature that was at ninety degrees, and the bologna and banana sandwiches were made early that morning. By the way, we didn't have one of those things called a cooler. So, by the time we were able to eat, the bananas had turned black, and I'm not so sure, but the bologna was probably green. Apparently, it didn't kill any of us, as we all lived to adulthood.

Well as anyone knows, when you have a small child on a trip with you, you are going to do what you have to do when you hear, "I've got to pee!" My mother was thinking ahead when she thought to bring along the little chamber-pot. My little brother relieved himself in the pot, and so there was no mishap, like turning the pot over by someone, mother went to the back of the truck with pot in hand and threw its contents out the back of the truck.

Needless to say, the truck causes a vacuum while in motion, and I think every drop came right back into the truck giving us all a mini shower to say the least.

The trip back home was a lot more fun, we looked like a bunch of lobsters that were just taken out of a pot of boiling water. We didn't have that fancy suntan lotion or umbrella to get out of the sun. By the time, we realized we had been in the sun too long, it was too late and we were fried. You have never seen a more miserable bunch than we were.

But, you know looking back, if I had it to do all over again with the pee shower and getting blistered, I would say, "No way."

A few Winstead kids; (left to right) back row: Cecil, Barbara, Me, Floyd; front row: Rusty, (our dog) and Don.

(Photo Courtesy of Winstead Family ©2017)

She's Funny You Know

My brother Don and I went to stay a couple of weeks with our Uncle Joe and Aunt Lis and their children in Virginia. Just the idea of going somewhere different was exciting enough, but to go to another state seemed like a big deal for sure. Our Aunt Lis always made us feel welcomed and a little more so than Uncle Joe did. Uncle Joe seemed to just tolerate us as long as we worked and did all the chores he assigned us each day. I must say, there were dividends when we stayed with them as they lived in the back of and above their country store. There were soda pops and candy staring you in the face all day, and Aunt Lis was very generous. I remember a soda pop that was my favorite, a strawberry flavor. I don't remember the name of it, but I remember how good it was and how many of them I would drink in a day depended on how many I could charm my Aunt Lis or my cousin Jeannette out of.

Train tracks ran down right beside the store. It was always fun to see the streamliner locomotive that was the Amtrak Silver Meteor. The Silver Meteor would come by at such a speed that it passed within seconds. The freight trains that would pass were a different story, as they would have three or four big black engines that would be running at the same time in order to pull an enormous number of cars that had to total over a hundred and loaded with everything under the sun. My brother Don and I would put a penny on the track so that when the train ran over it, it would double in size, and sometimes we would spend a half-hour trying to find the penny after the train had gone by.

I remember sleeping upstairs and on the same side of the house the tracks were on. It must have been the first time I spent the night with my aunt and uncle and I was probably around nine years old. I was asleep in a very dark and strange place when this terrific whistle and rumbling noise that was the train, sounded as if it was coming right through the bedroom. The whole house shook as if an earthquake was bringing down the entire structure. Frightened out of my mind, and almost shaken out of the bed, I screamed out for my Aunt Lis and she came and assured me that everything was ok.

The tracks ran north and south, and I think about every thirty minutes a train was going one way or the other. I don't think Don and I got a lot of sleep on our first night out of state.

A couple of days later, my Aunt Lis told Don and I to go with her to her neighbor's house, the home of Mrs. Ferguson, which was just down the road about two hundred yards. As we were walking along, Aunt Lis told us to behave ourselves because Mrs. Ferguson was kind of funny when it came to children. As we approached the neighbor's home, we saw Mrs. Ferguson out in her yard tinkering about with a potted plant stand. After we had been standing there awhile, I heard this chopping sound behind us and I turned to find my little brother Don, with an axe, to which he was testing its cutting ability on one of Mrs. Ferguson's new Japanese maple trees. To my aunt's horror she screamed at Don to put the axe down, and then she apologized to Mrs. Ferguson and grabbed Don by the hand and said, "Let's go." On our way back, she smacked Don on the backside and exclaimed, "Didn't I tell you that she was funny?!"

Don said that he didn't think she was all that funny as nobody was even laughing!

I think that I knew what Aunt Lis meant, but I think Don must have misconstrued the word funny somewhere in the true context in which it was meant.

My brother Floyd and our Uncle Joe (William Jody Winstead).

(Photo Courtesy of Winstead Family ©2017)

One Footnote, Filed

One day I was playing at the tool shed when I came across an old file, you know just a pointed handle on one end. That gave me an idea that if I sharpened it some, that I could throw it like a knife and it would stick in whatever it hit. We had a sharpening wheel to sharpen other tools like axes, hoe's and such. I sharpened the point of that handle so that it was like an ice pick. I threw it a few successful times and it found its mark on the side of the barn, however more times than not, it would just bounce off and fall to the ground. So, I decided that throwing it at that distance the odds were against me in hitting my target, so I started locating targets on the ground in which I was much closer to and the file would not have to flip at all. Then I saw a small piece of paper on the ground that made a great target. I drew back over my right shoulder and with a thrust, threw the file at the piece of paper but instead of spearing the paper, I stuck that file right into the top of my foot.

My mother again came to my aid using the same first aid technique with the kerosene and paper bag remedy as she had before. God blessed us, as she was a wife, mother, cook, housekeeper, nurse, and all the things that made her a great and wonderful woman, and especially a great mother.

A larger and sharper file like this one is what went into my foot.

(Photo Courtesy of Jimmy Winstead ©2017)

Cigar Sick

When I was somewhere around ten or eleven years old my brother, Richard, was home from the army and was staying with us. One day my daddy and mother went to town and left my sisters, Barbara and Frances, me and my younger brothers, Don and Terry at home. My mother gave us instructions about the chores we were to perform while they were away. One of the chores for Frances and I were to get the clothes off the clothesline and bring them into the house. The only thing that I was to do was to hold the basket for Frances to put the clothes in. But wait, let's back up a little.

A little earlier that morning I happened to see a small box of Cuban, Rum Crook cigars on the mantel over the fireplace that my brother Richard had left there. Unable to resist the temptation that soared through my mind to be grown, and a man if you will. I removed one of the cigars from the brightly colored box and slid it into my pocket. I slipped through the kitchen to acquire a match, so that I could saunter on out behind the barn and with each step I could fill myself growing taller with the anticipation of lighting that cigar and blowing a bluish cloud of smoke from my lips.

Soon, I'm clear and undetected and the much-anticipated time is here, and I intend to completely bathe in this moment of adulthood. I light the cigar and puff a couple of times to get it going good. Then I moved it over into the corner of my mouth which made me look real cool, like Edward G. Robinson, or a gangster character from the movies. I'm caught up in the moment, and puff away on the cigar. I actually smoked that cigar right down to the point where I actually couldn't hold it in my lips without burning them.

I started back to the house when I heard my sister Frances call me. At that moment, I realized that something was very wrong with me. I had trouble walking in a straight line, and I didn't feel so good either. Within a few moments, I was there with Frances to get the clothes off the line. With each passing moment, I got sicker and drunker. Frances asked me what was wrong with me, and I told her what I had done. She advised me I had better get straightened out before our parents got back. She said, "You think you are sick now and can't walk, wait till Mother finds out what you did, you want be able to sit either." I knew she was telling the truth, but I was so sick, and my head was spinning around about a thousand RPM's. Frances looked at me and said, "Jimmy, your face is green." I have no doubt that she was telling the truth as I felt green. Finally, I couldn't stand anymore, so I laid on the ground beneath the clothesline. Frances kept trying to encourage me to get up before Daddy and Mother returned, but to no avail.

Good fortune, luck or a guardian angel just happened to be there for me that day, because our parents were gone a lot longer than we anticipated and I had time to recover from one of the worst feelings I ever had as a child that tried to be too big for his britches.

Don (holding a white cat), Frances and me.

(Photo Courtesy of Winstead Family ©2017)

Bottoms Up

Back in the days of my early childhood, money was something I rarely possessed. I knew what it was but seldom did I have a cent to my name. But on one bright and sunshiny day my older brother, Cecil and I, were walking along the dirt road that bordered our house when we were living on the Fletcher Farm. As we were walking along, a sparkle of light reflected off of something on the ground. As I got closer, I was able to see that there in front of me, laid the treasure of a bright and shiny Jefferson nickel. Excited with my discovery, I moved to pick it up and at the same moment my brother tried to grab the nickel before I could get it. I happened to be closer and fortunate enough, to retrieve the coin right out from under his hand. Of course, a struggle and argument ensued over who saw it first.

Our father came along to see the struggle for possession and called a halt to the situation. We both pled our case that we had seen the nickel first, but my father wanting to be fair about it, told us to go to the store together and buy something that we could divide and therefore we could share the found treasure equally. I felt that would be fair and Cecil also agreed that we would go to the store and pick an item that would give us the maximum amount of product for the price. We went through a list of items from bubblegum, candy, cookies and so on until we decided that it was so hot that day, that a nice cold Pepsi Cola would be just the ticket to quench our thirst after the long and dusty walk to the store.

We reached Taylor's Store and straight to the Pepsi cooler we went. After retrieving that wonderful bottle of cold and wet delight, I handed the clerk the nickel and a penny tax that our father had so generously donated to our cause. Cecil went over to the bottle opener that was on the side of the cooler and popped the cap. I remember licking my lips at the sound of the fizz the Pepsi made when the pressure was released.

Cecil turned the bottle up and began gulping large amounts of Pepsi. As we left the store he continued gulping and gulping to the point I could see that more than half was already consumed by my loving and sharing brother. I quickly objected to his shenanigans but to no avail. When he had sucked the very last drop from the bottle, he handed the empty bottle to me. I can't tell you how disappointed I was that I didn't get a drop of that Pepsi Cola. I demanded that he explain just why he drank my half of the Pepsi. His explanation was that his half was on the bottom and my half was in the way of him getting his. Needless to say, that explanation was unacceptable reasoning and I was not going to stand for it.

When we reached home, I went to Father and told him what Cecil had done. He called Cecil and handed him six cents and told him to run as fast as his little legs could carry him to Taylor's Store and purchase a Pepsi Cola, unopened, and return as quick as he could and give the Pepsi to me. Then he was instructed to watch me drink every swallow until it was gone. Cecil did just like Dad told him to. That Pepsi was wonderful!

Taylor's Store near the Fletcher farm.

(Photo Courtesy of Jimmy Winstead ©2017)

Forgotten in Cotton

Just outside of Nashville N.C., we lived on yet, another farm known as the Noah farm. It was not a big farm so sometimes we had time to make a little money by helping some of the larger farmers.

A farmer, for whom I won't call his name, came to the house and asked my father if some of his kids could go to his farm and chop the grass out of his cotton. He said that he would pay a day's wages for a day's work. My father agreed for my brother Don and myself to go and work for him. The next day the man came and picked us up on a truck and drove us a long way back in a field, so far back that the sun sat between where we were at and home. Well maybe not that far, but it was some ways back there.

When we arrived at the field, the man told us to get a hoe out the back of the truck and to start chopping the grass out of the cotton. So, now we are on the first row of cotton chopping away when we heard the man start the truck and drive away. We thought that the man was leaving for just a short while so we continued chopping the grass out like we were told.

The sun was getting up pretty high and it was getting hotter and hotter. The man didn't leave us any water, food or any indication when he would return, so we just kept working. Don said that he was really thirsty and I was feeling it too. An old trick to keep your mouth from being so dry, is to find a small smooth stone and put it in your mouth. We continued working until it was late in the evening without water or food. Finally, the man returned and drove us back home. When we arrived home, we got out of the truck and waited for the man to pay us, but instead of paying us, he said that he wanted us to work the next day and he would pay us then. Then he just drove away leaving us standing in the yard. My dad came out and saw us standing there with empty hands. We told him that we didn't want to go back there to work. He asked us why, and we told him what happened, no money, no water, and no food.

I don't think I had ever seen my dad as mad at someone as he was that man. Dad went in the house, and told me to go get in the car. Pretty soon he was back, and we were on our way to the man's house that we had worked for. When we arrived at the man's house, Dad told me to stay in the car. I remember Dad owned a little pistol, and I'm not too sure that he didn't have it with him when he banged on the man's front door. I can tell you this, Dad let the man in no uncertain terms know how he felt about how he had treated us. I truly think Dad scared the crap out of the man. I could hear a word here and there, but all I know is, Dad put his finger in the man's face more than once, and I'm sure he swore at him quite a few times.

Dad came back with the money the man owed us, and I think he may have gotten a little extra, because he told me on our way back home that the man had to pay a little interest. At that time, I didn't understand what he meant, but Mother explained it to me later when I asked her what Dad meant. Needless to say, we never worked for that guy again.

North Carolina cotton.

(Photo Courtesy of Jimmy Winstead ©2017)

Early Bird Gets the Worm

Living on the farm, we had a few barnyard animals, and in particular a couple of big white roosters. Now, for those that have always lived in the city, and have never been around farm animals may not know that some roosters will attack you when you are in their territory. Some roosters are worse than others, and the two that we had were the worst. On several occasions, I have seen my mother run them off the porch with a broom because when she would start out the door, one or both would attack her. Roosters have very sharp spurs on their legs and will jump up in the air and thrust them at you and can cause serious cuts to a person or another animal.

My brother Don was just about five at the time, and I think I had been charged with keeping an eye on him while he was out in the yard playing. Don went over to the barn shelter and said that he had to pee. I told him to go under the barn shelter and do his thing. Well in a matter of seconds I heard him screaming. I ran under the shelter and saw a big white rooster trying to get Don's privates. The rooster kept lunging at Don, and Don kept trying to get away. I saw a rope hanging on a nail, so I grabbed the rope. The rope had a knot in the end of it so, I swung the rope around and around and caught the roosters neck with the rope, then I jerked it real hard, jerking the rooster away from Don. After getting Don to safety, I looked back to see where the rooster was at and saw him fluttering around on the ground. Within seconds, the old white rooster was dead.

I was a little afraid to go tell my mom that I had killed the rooster, but I went and told her anyway. To my surprise, after I told her why and how I came to kill him, she was not upset at all with me. She told me to go get him and put him on the back porch and that she would cook and make a chicken stew out of that mean ole rascal.

A Rattle for My Baby Brother
(As told by Mary Frances Winstead Morris)

When we were living on the Noah farm near Nashville, and I was about twelve years old, I would go and pick blackberries with my mother. We would pick the blackberries, for what seemed like hours. We would go home, wash them and sort out any leaves or trash that might have accidently fallen in them. Mother would let them air dry and then we would put them in quart jars and put a jar lid on them to keep them fresh. Then I would go about the neighborhood and sell the jars of blackberries. I can't remember how much I sold them for, but it was not very much I'm sure. This was a way to make a little change to buy me something whenever we went to town.

We didn't go to town very often, but when we did, I remember how excited it was to go and look into the shop windows at all the pretty stuff on display. How my mind would wonder off into another world where I was wearing those beautiful dresses and shoes. I would forget for a moment that in reality I was wearing a feed sack dress that my mother had made, and my feet were bare.

But on this day, I had some money to buy me whatever the amount of money would buy me. We of course didn't shop at the high dollar boutiques, we shopped at the five and dime store. When you have just a little money, and not a lot of opportunities to go shopping, you take your time and try and find just the right thing. I looked at this and that and saw things that cost more than what I had until I saw a baby rattle. It was like the perfect thing to buy, but not for me, but for my baby brother Terry. I was so pleased that I was able to buy him something I could hardly wait to get home to give it to him.

When we did get home, I ran inside and saw Terry sitting on the floor. I got on my knees and removed the rattle from the paper bag. I slowly handed the rattle to Terry and his eyes lit up. I said, "Look what your sister bought you." Terry reached out taking it from my hand and smiled, at that very moment I knew that all the work and time I had put into making that little bit of money had paid off more than I ever thought it could.

My sister, Frances.

(Photo Courtesy of Winstead Family ©2017)

Neighbor Nuisances

We were able to catch the school bus in front of our house every day that school was in session. Schools were still segregated at that time and the buses for each school stopped there in order to pick up students. I don't think up until that particular day had we had any problems out of the people that lived down the dirt road beside our house, but on that day, things changed completely.

While we were waiting for our school bus that morning, my sisters, Frances and Barbara were standing there talking when the neighbor, which was about fourteen years old was waiting for his school bus, looked over at my sister Frances and made a very lude remark to her. Well, one thing you didn't do back then or even now, is to mess with one of the brothers or sisters of the Winstead clan. I won't call this young man's name, but that is where he clearly messed up by saying the dirty words to Frances.

My sister Barbara walked toward him and he picked up a rock and hit her in her stomach. Barbara never slowed up, until she was close enough to deck him in the nose knocking him to the ground. About that time, his bus showed up and our bus pulled up right behind it. Every time he would get up, Barbara would knock him back down. The kids on his bus were laughing at this young man getting his butt handed to him by a young girl, and the kids on our bus were cheering her on.

Pretty soon I think he realized his only choice to get relief from the pounding he was getting was to somehow get on his bus. But every time he made that attempt, Barbara knocked him down. Finally, he was able to get away and jump in the bus. The punishment didn't stop there, we could hear the kids on his bus teasing him about how this little young girl had whooped his butt. Needless to say, he never made the same mistake of saying something ugly or vulgar to my sisters again.

My sisters, Frances and Barbara.

(Photo Courtesy of Winstead Family ©2017)

Going to Get My Shotgun

Another instance that happened while we were at the Noah farm, involved the same neighbors living down the dirt road. Just to fill you in on what type of folks they were, I'll tell you some of the things that I know to have happened in the short time we lived there.

One thing that stuck out in my mind was the time the husband chased his naked wife across a plowed field with an axe. Another time, the husband threw their infant baby across the road and then went to smother it to death with his coat until his older son stabbed him in the back with a butcher knife. Then one early morning, the wife threw boiling water on her husband while he was still drunk in the bed.

I can't say if these people were mean or just plain crazy. But any way you look at it, they were not your average family.

Now I'm not saying that me and my brothers didn't have a little mischievous blood in us, but I don't think that we were mean to anyone. We played tricks on each other once in a while, but just for fun, but one night we decided to play a trick on the wrong person. You got it right, the neighbor down the dirt road.

Well, this is the way it went on that hot summer night as my brothers, Cecil, Don and myself, sat on top of a shelter that was between two tobacco barns. My brother Cecil would sometimes tell me and Don stories that he would just make up as he went, and most of the time they would be very interesting. I think he had a great imagination, and was very talented when he told us stories that captured our imagination.

We would sit on the barn shelter where it was quiet and you could get a little breeze on those hot summer nights. Well, on that particular night we were enjoying one of Cecil's adventurous tales when Cecil spotted a light in the distance coming down the dirt road. The barn shelter was within ten feet of the road, and we had a perfect view of anything that was going or coming down the road.

I think Cecil recognized at once that it was the neighbor man from down the road. The man was obviously drunk and was riding a bicycle with a flashlight attached to the handlebars, and that light went from one side of the road to the other. Every now and then you would hear him curse, or mumble something and he was no doubt having trouble controlling the bicycle.

Cecil said, "I have a good idea, when he gets here to the shelter, we will bang our feet on this tin top and scare him." So, when he was right there at the shelter we banged our feet on that tin top as loud as we could. Sure enough, it scared the crap out of him and he fell off the bicycle. Needless to say, we thought it was funny and we were laughing like crazy until he got back to his feet and tried to get back on the bicycle, but ended up dragging it instead of rolling it. Then in a very angry voice declared that he was going home to get his shotgun, and kill somebody on that barn shelter.

Cecil said that we better get out of there, because he was just crazy enough to do it. So, we got off the shelter and ran to the house. In a few minutes, we heard a shotgun blasting the shelter where we had just left. After that, I don't think we fooled around with trying to scare our crazy neighbor anymore.

Parachute Drop

When I was about twelve years old, we lived outside of Nashville, N.C. on a farm known as the Boone Farm. My brother Don was about ten years old so he pretty much followed me around to play our army and cowboy games.

On one of those days we decided to play a game I called, airborne, which meant jumping out of a plane which we, of course, did not have at our disposal. What we did have was young, creative enthusiasm and a wild imagination. So, like any adventurous young boy, we looked for something that could be used for a parachute and there it was, a canvas tarp about a ten-foot square, perfect.

Now all we needed was an airplane. No problem, we were already in it, the barn. We figured, or maybe it was just me that figured, that if each of us held a corner of the tarp in each hand and we jumped from the loft of the barn, which was probably about forty feet from the ground, that the air would gather under the tarp bringing us softly and gently to the landing zone.

So now the plan had come together, and it was time to test the theory of that plan. I don't know about Don, but I had grown a little nervous about situation, but I would never let on for a moment to my little brother that I was scared.

Now the time had come to jump. Don and I were standing at the plane door waiting for the red flashing light and orders from the sergeant to bail out. I looked at Don and he looked as calm and cool as a cucumber. I think that because I was not showing any signs of chickening out, that he thought, it must be ok to jump.

So now, I tell him that we will jump at the count of three, and he just nods ok. Then at the count of three, I jumped, but Don hesitated to jump at the same time. This was a 'Houston, we have a problem' moment. I fell at 35 feet per second, landing on my knees and chest, relieving me of any air that was in my lungs. But then a split second later, Don crash landed right on top of me. All I can remember from that very moment was Don saying, "I broke my back!" I couldn't say anything for a couple of minutes.

I think we deserted from the airborne on that day. Our jumping days were over and thank God, we never tried that again.

Now for those that don't think you have a guardian angel, think again. We walked away from that crash landing without a scratch or broken bone. Once I had my breath back, and Don realized that he had not broken his back, we went on to other things to do for the rest of the day, and probably just as crazy as the parachute drop.

The Boone Farm barn that my brother Don and I jumped out of. Photo taken in 2017.

(Photo by Jimmy Winstead ©2017)

I Found My Thrill on Taylor's Hill

At the age of around thirteen years old, we lived in a community near the city limits of Rocky Mount, N.C., called Taylor's Hill. It was a pretty old and run down area with houses that still did not have indoor plumbing, and our house was no exception. The house had just four rooms, a kitchen, a living room and two bedrooms.

We indeed lived on the wrong side of the tracks as the railroad yard was just beyond our house, and the sound of shifting train cars banging day and night was the norm.

One fall evening I was walking down by a creek that was about two hundred yards behind our house. Suddenly I heard a cry for help. I looked in the direction of the sound to see two young boys. Both boys had fallen off a homemade raft into the cold and muddy creek. I ran to the bank of the creek to find that neither boy could swim and were frantically trying to get to land. I was a pretty good swimmer so I waded out into the creek and grabbed ahold of one of the boys and I remember the look of fear in his eyes. I pulled him ashore and went back for the other boy, which by this time had gone past where we were at. I was able to swim out to him. He was submerged all but back of his jacket and I pulled him up and above the water where he was able to get a breath. After sputtering and coughing I heard him take a deep breath. I pulled him with all my might to reach the bank of the creek. To my relief, I touched the bottom and walked out of the creek with the boy in tow.

Needless to say, it was cold and the water had soaked through our clothes and we were all shivering pretty good by now. I hustled the boys back to our house and let them warm by the heater. I found out where they lived which was just a short distance from our house. Back then we did not have a phone, so calling their parents was not an option. Just to make sure they got home safe, I walked to their house with them.

When we reached their front door, the boy's mom came to the door and asked why they were so wet. After explaining to her their misfortune, and how I had pulled them from the creek, she scolded them and told me I had better get back to my own house and then closed the door in my face.

On my way back home, I think my feelings were a bit frazzled when she showed no appreciation for me saving the lives of her two children. I wondered after that day if she might have thought I was responsible for them being at the creek in the first place. Nevertheless, the main thing was that I was glad that I was there at that time and the boys were safe now.

My Beautiful Corn, Destroyed

Still at Taylor's Hill, more adventures were to come. Not a lot of land went with the house we lived in, but my father always found enough land to plant a garden. He took pride in his ability to plant and grow a sufficient amount of vegetables to get us through the winter months.

On this particular day of planting, I asked my father if I could plant something in the garden. He told me if I planted anything, I would be responsible in keeping the grass and weeds out, and make sure it had plenty water. I agreed to the terms and I was given some seed corn. I didn't have a plow, so I used a hoe to furrow the rows for my corn. I of course asked my father for advice on how deep I should plant my corn, and he was very helpful with both his advice and suggestions on how much fertilizer and soda to add when the time was right.

I wanted my father to be proud of my corn crop, so every day, I weeded, and watered, and pampered forty stalks of beautiful tall green corn. When my father saw how nice my corn looked, he indeed told me that he was very proud of how I had stuck to taking care of it and that my corn was as pretty as any he had ever grown. I'll tell you, my chest swelled, and it made me just as proud.

Dad was not a real tall man, but to see that corn standing three feet above his head was a sight to see.

As the corn matured, nice healthy ears appeared on my corn and the excitement grew in me that before too long, our family would be enjoying some of my sweet corn for dinner.

Just a few days later, my family and I had gone somewhere for the day. When we returned home I went around to the back of the house to water my corn, and there lying on the ground was every stalk of my corn, cut off at the ground. Not only had it been chopped down, but it was stripped of the ears of corn and strewn about the garden as though a tornado had struck. Most all of the ears of corn were too young to use, but I guess that didn't matter to the one that destroyed it.

We asked our neighbors if they had seen anyone in our garden, and one of our neighbors said that they saw a young boy about my age with a machete cutting the corn down, but they thought it was me. We never found out who was responsible for the dirty deed, or why.

Moms Are Smarter Than You Think

Growing up in a large family is great, and you think that because you are one of many you just might slide something past your sweet, dear Mom. But, in fact by the time I came along, my mom had pretty much learned all the little tricks that my older siblings had tried to get away with.

I must have thought that I was a little smarter than the rest because I was a teenager and I knew everything like most teens do. Well, I was soon to find out just who was the smarter of the two, Mom or me.

It was early one school morning when I prepared to skip school in favor of going swimming with some of my, also smarter, teenage friends to a sand pit where the water was like the lagoon in the Blue Lagoon movie. Right in the middle of the pond was a white mound of sand, the perfect place to go swimming.

The morning of the planned holiday was beautiful. The sun was shining and temperatures were above average. I was excited because this was the first time I had ever skipped school and I was proving to my friends that I was just as brave as any of them. Now I just had to figure a way to get my swimming trunks and towel out of the house without being caught. The first thing I did was put on my trunks on under my pants. Then I wrapped a towel around my waist and then put my shirt over that. I waited till I saw my mom in the kitchen cleaning up the breakfast dishes. I quickly walked over to her, kissed her on the cheek, and disappeared out the door. Wow, am I smart or what? She never suspected a thing.

Now I go and meet up with my school skipping buddies at the corner drug store. Soon all six of us were there and loaded into a 1958 Chevy. Off we went to our day of leisure and fun in the sun. After arriving at our destination of intent, off came the pants and shirts and into that wonderful pool of sweet delight. The pond, or better known as the sand pit was in a secluded area hidden from public eyes, so all day we enjoyed our private swim club.

After pretty much a full day of splashing, dunking and swimming, it was time we got out of the water so our trunks could dry and then we could put them back on under our pants.

Right on time, I arrived home just like every other school day with books in hand and a cheerful hello to my mother. I went to my room and got the towel and trunks off and put my trunks back in the dresser drawers, and put the towel in the clothes hamper. Well, I thought that went very well and no one was the wiser. I was feeling pretty dog gone good until my mother asked the inquisitive and unexpected question, "Why didn't you go to school today?" Now I'm standing there like a deer in the headlights completely off guard.

Now let me clue you in on something. Past experience told me not to try and lie to Mother because she already knew the truth before she asked but if you decided to chance it, well you were playing with fire. Now I'm squirming like a worm on a hot stove, so I answered the question with a question, "What makes you think I didn't go to school?"

Mother squinted her eyes a bit as she came closer to me and said, "Your nose and cheeks didn't get sunburned in a classroom, did they?" At that moment, I think my face probably turned another shade of red, but I confessed because I knew the jig was up, and my mom was smarter than me.

My mother told me that she was glad I told her the truth, but that didn't mean that it was ok. She never punished me for it or mentioned it again. Whew!

Nobody but Grandma

Going Fishing

My grandmother had come from Raleigh to spend a couple of weeks with us. Grandma wanted to go fishing at the creek behind the house where I pulled the two boys from the water in the Taylor's Hill area.

She sat on the backdoor steps prepping her cane pole with a line, sinker and cork bobber. My brother Don and I always hated for her to come and stay because I think she hated kids. If we whistled anywhere around her, even a low whistling tune, she would shout out for us to stop that dag-dem whistling, because it goes right through her head.

On that day, while she was preparing to go fishing, she was sitting on the back porch getting her fishing pole ready. Don and I went out the back door to play in the yard and stepped over her fishing pole. Grandma yelled at us to come back there and to step backwards over her pole, because according to her, it was bad luck to step over someone's fishing pole before they went fishing. Holding our comments to ourselves, we just did what she wanted and stepped backwards over her fishing pole. Later Don said, "Too bad she won't going hunting and had her shotgun laying there instead."

Waiting on Help

Our grandma was a tough old lady and would let you know with no uncertain terms how she felt about any situation that might arise. One instance that happened was when we lived across from a little grocery store in the Taylor's Hill area in Rocky Mount on the Arlington Street Extension. One day Grandma told me to go with her across the street to the store. So off we go and soon we were standing inside. My grandma backed up against the ice-cream box and waited for the proprietor to wait on her. For a good little while, Grandma stood there waiting and watching as she would see the lady that owned the store, walk back and forth, straightening things on the shelves, dusting, and then she went to the back room and then returned. After a long wait, the owner came by and asked my grandma if she could help her. My grandma said with sharp tone, "Well, I'm not leaning on this ice-cream box just to cool my ass!"

Tough Beef

One night my mother had prepared some beef stew, and as always it seemed as if my grandmother would find fault with something. My brother Don was seated beside Grandma, and seemed to be pleased with his meal as well as the rest of us. After a few minutes of tranquility and family bonding, my dear old grandma was chewing on a piece of the beef that was in her stew. She reached up and removed the piece of tough beef from her mouth and placed it on Don's plate and told him to eat it, that she couldn't chew it. You may as well have thrown a snake in his plate. Don's eyes were the size of saucers and he had a frantic expression was on his face. At that moment, I think Don was so flabbergasted, he didn't know what to say. My mother came to his rescue by jumping up and removing Don's plate. She told my grandma not to put food in somebody's plate that she has been chewing on. Grandma said, "Well I know his teeth are better than mine, and I didn't want to waste food."

Grandma, Sally Alma Leona Warbritton Gardner, my mothers' mother.

(Photo courtesy of Winstead Family ©2017)

A Snow Man?
(As told to me by Floyd E. Winstead)

My brother, Floyd, told me of an exciting adventure he and two of our older brothers
experienced when they were very young boys. Like most young boys, they used their imagination when it came to playing games. When you were poor, you made do with what you had whether it was food, clothes or toys. Your imagination was a very handy tool to possess, and most adults realized the fact that children back in those days used it more than they do today.

Daddy had made my brothers a water mill. For those that don't know what a water mill is, it's made from corn stalks and corn cobs, plus reeds or whatever is available. You put the water mill in a stream or creek. In their case, it was put in a stream that branched off of a creek, very far in the woods behind the house.

Richard Winstead

(Photo Courtesy of Winstead Family ©2017)

While playing with the water mill, Floyd said that he looked up and from across the creek, and coming toward them through a very thick briar patch, was this very large creature that resembled a snow man. He said the thing was white all over, very tall and had big black eyes. Floyd said that he could hear the leaves moving beneath the creature, but it was if it was almost floating, and it was able to penetrate the thick brush and briars with ease. He said he called out to our brothers, Pete and Richard and pointed at the creature to warn them that it was coming at them. Both Richard and Pete dropped what they were doing and high-tailed it out of there, leaving him to fend for himself, but that was only for a split second because he was right on their tails. Floyd said that he never looked back in fear that the creature might be right behind him.

Floyd and our mother, Minnie.

(Photo Courtesy of Winstead Family ©2017)

They all made it back home and in an exhausted state, fell upon the porch while screaming for mother. My mother was a pretty good judge when it came to finding out if you were telling the truth or not, so before you told her a lie, you better think of the consequences if she found you out. Mother came to see what all the commotion was about and saw nothing that warranted their behavior, but did scold them for being so late coming home.

They avoided that area for a couple of weeks or until their memories of the 'Snow Man' had faded. Not to say they didn't think about it from time to time, and occasionally look over their shoulders to make sure they were alone.

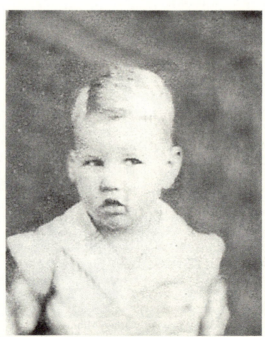

My brother 'Pete' (Raymond Cedrick Winstead).

(Photo Courtesy of Winstead Family ©2017)

In the Mood

We lived in an area called Sunset Hills in Rocky Mount, which was just a middle-class community of working people. My brother Terry was around eight or nine years old, and had a friend that lived across from us that was about the same age. I can't remember his friend's name, but I remember that he had to take piano lessons. Sometimes Terry would be over there when he was having his lesson and would watch as the young boy was learning how to play under the watchful eye of his teacher. I have no idea how long the lessons lasted, but I do know that terry took an interest in playing the piano. More than once he came home and told me that he was over at the neighbor's house playing the piano. I figured he had learned Chop Sticks or Mary Had a Little Lamb. This went on for just a short time before Terry was leaving the neighbor's house and saw me in our yard and hollered over at me, "Hey Jimmy, you want to hear me play the piano?"

I said, "Sure, I'll come over to hear you." So, I went over and stood at the front screen door where I could hear.

Terry sat down at the piano and placed both hands on the keys, and very much to my surprise, started playing a foot tapping tune called, In the Mood. I almost fell off the porch from the shock. I had no idea he knew how to play anything, and play it so well.

The mother of the little boy that was taking lessons said that she was amazed at how quick terry had picked up the art of playing the piano. She also said that she wished her son could play as good as Terry without taking the first lesson, because he learned how to play by ear.

So, from the early age of eight or nine, Terry has been playing the piano, and has been in the music business for many, many years. He can still tickle the old ivories.

Terry Winstead

(Photo Courtesy of Terry Winstead ©2017)

My First Time
(As told to me by Terry D. Winstead)

I had almost forgotten about something that happened after I was an adult, until my youngest brother brought it to my attention just the other day.

I can't remember how old Terry was at the time, but he was at little league baseball practice at one of the ball parks in Rocky Mount, N.C when my brother Don and I went to pick him up. I started driving away from the park when Terry asked me why we were going in that direction, I told him that it was a surprise for him.

Terry told me that when I told him it was a surprise for him, he thought maybe I was going to Dairy Queen to buy him some ice cream. He said that he was not prepared for the surprise I had waiting for him when we pulled up to the Rocky Mount Municipal Airport. He thought that maybe I took him out there just to watch the planes land and take off, but never did he think he would get to go up in one of them.

I had pre-arranged the whole thing, so when we got there the pilot came right on out and we all loaded up and took off.

Terry told me that the airplane ride was one of his most memorable experiences, and one of the most exciting things that happened to him at that age. Terry said that when the pilot turned the plane, it seemed to always be turning to his left and that was the side of the plane he was sitting on. He said that he could look almost straight down and he was afraid that the window might break out and he would fall out. So, every time the plane turned left, Terry said that he would grab Don's shirt so in case the window didn't hold, maybe Don's shirt would.

I'm so glad Terry reminded me of that day. At the time when you do something like that, you don't think it means a lot, but when I listened to Terry give his account of that day, I knew that even though it was just a local flight around the county, it meant a lot to a little boy taking his first air plane ride, and I got to be a part of it.

I wish my brother Don was here to share these memories, God bless his soul.

Me and Terry on his high school graduation day.

(Photo Courtesy of Winstead Family ©2017)

A Mighty Snore

Several years ago, my brother Don and I went on one of our fishing trips. We usually went deep-sea fishing, which in itself would take up an entire day. The boat would always leave out early in the morning and return late that evening. For that reason, and of course factor in that we lived so far away, we would get a motel room so we could get up and be there in a matter of minutes.

I think on this particular trip we had pretty good luck fishing. Both of us were tired and pretty worn out from reeling in fish from the bottom of the ocean, or it sure seemed as if that's where they were.

That night after the fishing trip was over we were at the motel room, bushed, ready to take a shower and get some much-needed rest and sleep. About ten minutes after I got into my bed, Don got out of the shower and got into his bed. I thought to myself, now at last I can get some rest but I was 'WRONG,' as Don started snoring within twenty seconds after he fell into bed. I thought, "Oh my God," what a noise. You would think someone was riding a Harley Davidson around in our room. I'm not joking, I even placed my hand against the wall and it was vibrating like a heavy truck had just came through. There was no way I was going to go to sleep with that air hammer in the bed next to me, so I got out of bed and went over and shook him and told him to turn over the other way. He grunted something and continued to 'roar snore'. I shook him violently and tried to get him awake enough to understand what I was saying, but to no avail.

I thought, my Lord, I won't get any rest and definitely no sleep tonight unless I get him to shut up. After a few more attempts to wake him with no success, I went into the desperate mode. I pulled the covers off him and grabbed him by his ankles and dragged him off the bed and on to the floor where he continued as if nothing had changed. I thought, 'Well, there's just one more thing I know to try, and that's some cold water dashed in his face.' However, I figured that was a way to wake up everybody in the motel when the fight started, but what the heck, at least I won't be the only one not getting any sleep. So, I went over and emptied the water from the ice bucket into a plastic cup, and oh yeah, the water was ice cold. I went back over to where the rolling thunder was still going on and lifted the covers and threw the whole cup of water right in his crotch area.

The dragon is awake, and yes, he was pissed! A few, or let me rephrase that, a bunch of choice slang words came out of his mouth. I was prepared for whatever he intended to do about it, if it meant fighting or whatever. After he got over the shock and was able to at least be somewhat coherent, I was able to make him understand that nobody could sleep in that room except him with the noise he was making.

My final solution for a more restful night was to get another room, and I made sure it would be far away enough that his snoring wouldn't bother me.

The next morning, I went to his room to get the rest of my things. I kept a key to that room in case I needed something that I left in there. I tried to wake Don because we had to leave and get back home because I had to work a third shift with the police department that night. Every time I would shake him and tell him he needed to get up, he would tell me to leave him alone. I told Don that I had to work that night so I had to leave. My pleading fell on deaf ears, and he refused to get up. I was driving, so I finally told him that unless he was ready in the next fifteen minutes he could sleep the rest of the day because I would leave him there.

I went outside and waited for him. After fifteen minutes and not a second more, I got into my car and drove away and left 'Sleeping Beauty' there. When I got home I called his wife and explained to her what happened and why, she was a bit upset with both me and Don.

It was a couple of weeks before Don got over being mad at me, and finally called me. I asked him how he got home and he told me that he saw a couple of guys with Rocky Mount city tags on their car and asked them if he could ride back with them, and that was about an hour after I left. That boy sure was a lucky nut, if it had been me, someone would have to make a trip to get me. But it all worked out ok and we made more trips together, and I wish we could today.

I miss Don, a lot!

My brother Don, and myself.

(Photo Courtesy of Winstead Family ©2017)

Plant a Garden and They Will Come

Usually at harvest time we would have company call on us that we hadn't seen since the last harvest. My dad, Raymond, always had a large garden. The main reason being, he had a large family. Not only did he raise all varieties of vegetables, but we had fruit trees that produced apples, pears, peaches, plums and figs. My mother always canned a lot of vegetables and fruits and stored them in a pantry.

In the winter, we always harvested our hogs. My daddy had a smokehouse where he would make sugar cured hams, fresh shoulders, sausage, plus several other cuts of meat such as pork chops, and fat back. There were all different cuts of meat that hung in the smokehouse there for us to eat through-out the coming year.

We had a cow for fresh milk, buttermilk and would make freshly churned butter, and by the way, I got to do my share of the churning too. There were chickens for eating and for eggs, and by the time we had thinned out the flock of chickens for our Sunday dinners, the hens were hatching more chicks. The ole sow was having little piglets and mother was having more babies. Somehow it all seemed to work itself out and make sense.

I got a little side tracked from where I started, but as I was saying, we would get company we never heard from or saw until harvest time. Oh and by the way, they would show up just before lunch had been set on the table, and of course being the person my mother was, she would invite them to eat with us. Mother would get the same old answer, "Well Minnie, (Minnie was my mother), we didn't come to eat, we just happened to be in the area at this time so we decided to drop in to see you, but it sure does smell good. What is that, chicken I smell?"

Then after their guts were stuffed, the question always came up, "How did your garden turn out this year? What say we go have a look at your garden Raymond, bet it does look good, you always have a beautiful garden and plenty of it too." A not so subtle suggestion that we had more than we needed, so they would be more than willing to take it off our hands, you know so it wouldn't go to waste. My daddy had a very large variety of vegetables plus watermelons and cantaloupes, and I can tell you that none of our kin ever offered to help plant or harvest any of it but for themselves.

After filling their bellies and the trunk of their car, I would hear my mother say in a whisper, "See you again next year", as they were driving away.

Can We Ride the Horse?

One of our cousins, his wife, and their twin boys showed up one Sunday about lunch time and of course, pretty much invited themselves for lunch. I remember very clearly my mother saying to my dad that she had cooked just enough for our family that day.

I knew that when we had company in those days, the children had to wait until the adults had eaten before you were allowed to get to the table. After hearing my mother's comment to Dad about the amount of food there was, I knew that somehow, I was going to come up on the short end of the stick. Needless to say, my meal was limited to a few cold vegetables. We didn't have microwaves back then to re-warm the food as we cooked with a stove that used wood as fuel. To top it all off, I had to help my sister wash the dishes afterwards. And then, of course after filling their bellies, the cousins wanted to check out the garden.

Now, back to riding the horse…my dear little cute dressed cousins each had matching, little brown shorts, brown sandals, white socks and starched white shirts with brown bowties. Oh, my God, were they adorable! Now those twins were really cute and they even made me smile a bit, maybe even a little chuckle.

After our cousin and his wife had made their selections from our garden, they sat with my mother and dad in the shade on our front porch.

Meanwhile, it was left to me to entertain my little twin cousins. So being a good host and being in charge of entertainment, I directed them to *my* playground, 'the farm'. I escorted them down to the stables, not where we had expensive riding horses, but where we had working mules. One of the twins, I can't remember which one, asked me if they could ride the horse. "Well sure you can," I said, "I'll catch one for you, but you'll have to help". Mind you, it had rained for three days before, and along with the rain and the mud there was several days the mules had made their deposits. The muck was probably four to five inches deep in the outside stable yard.

I took the twins inside the barn and up the stairs to the hayloft. There was a door that opened to the outside from the upstairs hayloft and into the stable yard. I placed a rope around the waists of both of the twins and gave one of the twins the other end of the loop. I had both of them sit in the hayloft doorway and told them that I was going down the stairs to run the 'horse' out. When the twin with the looped rope saw the horse, he was to drop the loop around its neck and both should hold the rope tight so it wouldn't get away. I went down the stairs and ran out old 'Rackley', who was the largest and the most hardheaded mule you've ever seen and even I was a little afraid of him. I smacked him on his rump and out of there he went. Just like a real cowboy, my twin cousins dropped the rope around the mule's neck and they held tight. I was still standing inside the stable barn when from above me I saw two figures go airborne and then two figures being dragged through all that muck. Well old 'Rackley' couldn't go any further than the fence would allow him so he continued to drag them around and around through the stable yard until I held up an ear of corn, and he came back inside the barn to get it. Both of those boys smelled to high heaven and I don't think there was a dry or clean spot on them anywhere.

Feeling that the entertainment session had come to an end, I walked the boys back to the house where they found a seat on the back-porch steps. Both were crying and sounded like a couple of wailing calves in a hail storm. I warned them not to go inside, because my mother would give them something to really cry about if they did. I went inside and told their mother that her sons wanted her.

Their mother came out to find two little boys covered in crap and mud from head to toe. The look on her face was priceless, and I thought for several moments that I was going to get to see her throw-up. She led the boys out to the well, where they were stripped down to their under drawers and all. Buckets of deep, cold well water were drawn and poured on them, over and over again, time after time, and even in the summer that cold water would make your teeth chatter. They were dried off and rushed to their car, where they sped out of there not to be seen again for a few more years.

I thought my mother would be extremely upset and disappointed with me, but after they were gone, she just looked at me with a slight smile and twinkle in her eye and said, "Jimmy, what did you do?"

I just shrugged my shoulders and said, "They wanted to go for a ride and they got one."

Several years later, the boys' father was visiting my parents and I happened to be there. I asked him if he remembered that incident with the boys and the stable with the mule fiasco. His reply was, "A ten or fifteen-mile car ride with two stinking, naked boys and a crying, screaming wife is something you will never ever forget."

Rudolph Deans, the son of Tom Deans, is leading Betsy. Rackley, the hardheaded mule, is on the left.

(Photo Courtesy of Winstead Family ©2017)

A Bouquet for Their Mom

My big city, twin cousins were visiting us again, and as usual I had to try and entertain them while they were there because they were close to my age.

They may have been city smart, which I wasn't, but they were not country farm smart either. I was always amused at the questions they asked like, "Why is that pig on that other pigs back?" Or one good question was, "Which one of the cows gives the butter and which one gives the cheese?"

After a couple of hours playing around the barns and stables, I decided to take them on a safari through the corn fields and tobacco fields. I figured those pretty white shirts and shorts could use a little color. Oblivious that every time they rubbed against a tobacco leaf that it left a sticky residue called tobacco gum on their clothes, they followed me right in the thick of it all.

Floyd and Daddy topping tobacco.

(Photo Courtesy of Winstead Family ©2017)

Pretty soon it was time for us to go back to the house for dinner so I told the boys that it would be nice if they were to take their mother a bouquet of flowers. They said that they would if they had some. So being the good thoughtful cousin that I was, I told them that they could pick those beautiful flowers from atop the tobacco stalks. I said look at the beautiful pink and white flowers that you can get, as a matter of fact, get her an arm-full, she will love them. My cousins got real excited that they could have all the flowers they wanted and began breaking off the tobacco blooms. After each had an arm full, they hurried to the house to present them to their mother. When they came bearing gifts, their poor mom didn't know how to tell them that they had been tricked, and that the flowers they picked were nasty gummy dirty tobacco tops that the farmers pulled off and threw away.

Oh well, probably not the worst thing I've ever done, nor the worst thing that has ever happened to my cute, little cousins in the white shorts and shirts. Sorry guys.

My mother, Minnie and sister, Barbara with others getting the tobacco sorted and looped.

(Photo Courtesy of Winstead Family ©2017)

Ghost Bicycle?

Several years back, when my dad and mom were living, I was just sitting around talking with them about some of their experiences as children and early in their marriage, before they had children.

Minnie and Raymond Winstead

(Photo Courtesy of Winstead Family ©2017)

I've never had my mother or dad come right out and tell me a bald-faced lie, or if they were just kidding, they would admit that they were joking. On this occasion, they told me a story that was a little hard to swallow, but they both swore to me that it was true. Therefore, I will tell it as they told me, and you can make your own judgement. For me, I believe them, because knowing them like I did, it must have been true.

Both my mom and dad told the story, one would be telling something, and the other would chime in and finish their sentence.

My mom and dad had been married for a short time and were living with my dad's brother, Roy and his wife, Lessie. I don't remember where they lived at the time but they did say it was out in the country.

Uncle Roy and Aunt Lessie

(Photo Courtesy of Winstead Family ©2017)

They told me it was just about dusk and the four of them were sitting out on the front porch waiting for an occasional cool breeze to come by and cool them from the hot, steamy summer evening. They talked about how dry and hot it had been and how the crops were suffering from the lack of rain.

As they sat there, swatting mosquitoes and gnats and wiping sweat from their brow, they heard a noise to the left of them, sort of like a squeaking noise. A dirt road ran in front of the house and the house was on a hill. They knew it was not a car, but couldn't figure out what was making the noise. But pretty soon, coming up to the top of the hill was a bicycle. There was no one was on the bicycle, but the pedals were turning slow as if someone was having trouble getting up the hill. The bicycle passed right in front of them and then as it had reached the top of the hill, started to pick up speed. My mother said that my Uncle Roy jumped off the porch and took off after the bike as fast as he could run. Mother said that the bike picked up more speed down the hill and disappeared out of sight. My uncle was unable to catch the bike, and she said she was glad he didn't.

...And So, I Did

Somewhere between when I was four and five years old, my parents took all of us kids to the North Carolina State Fair in Raleigh. Back then, the N.C. State Fair was like Disneyland is to the kids of today. Very seldom did we get to go to a place where there were so many people and so many different things to see. I don't remember riding on any of the rides, but I do remember the excitement I felt as the music played and all the different colored lights glaring and blinking, as the rides roared and the ground trembled beneath my feet. At every turn, I experienced a different smell, including the Polish sausages with grilled onions and peppers, candy apples, cotton candy and even some I had never smelled or even seen before. Our dad bought a bag of roasted peanuts still in the shell and gave some to us. The peanuts were still warm and the aroma was fantastic.

We walked about the midway and took in all the free entertainment. The barkers were a little scary as they were in competition with each other to get you to come in and see their show. With their loud speakers blaring, they were blaring, "Right this way ladies and gentlemen, see the half-pig and half-sheep, just one tenth of a dollar or one thin dime". Some of the things that were on the inside that they were advertising seemed a little bizarre, and at my tender age I don't know if I really wanted to see them or not. I remember on one stage a man was swallowing swords, knives and assorted implements, and I thought that was pretty cool. Then there were the hoochie coochie shows, women strung out across the stage in very skimpy and somewhat revealing attire and that probably heightened my curiosity more than the half-pig, half-sheep. My mother grasped my shirtsleeve and a little bit of my skin with it, and told me to come along that we were going to see the half-pig, half-sheep show. As we walked inside the tent to see this weird wonder, I have never been so disappointed to see what I saw. Standing before us was a pig on one side of the stage, and on the other side was a sheep. Both animals had a sheet covering them from their waist back so all you could see was half of them, which was as advertised as, half-pig, half-sheep.

As we walked around the midway more and looked at more strange attractions, we stopped to look at something which I don't even remember what, but whatever it was I must have been intrigued with it because while I stood looking at it my parents and all my siblings moved on and through the crowd, without me. When I looked around to make a comment about the attraction, there were only strangers there to listen. I think a sudden jolt of fear raced through by entire body. I didn't want to act like I was scared, so I just sucked it up and began to walk in the direction I thought they might be.

After a few minutes, which I'm sure seemed like eternity, a police officer saw that I was alone and asked me if my mom and dad were lost. I said, "Yes sir, I don't know where they are."

The policeman was, or to me as a little kid, looked like he was ten feet tall. He smiled and told me that he would help me find them and for me not to worry. He asked me if I remembered what my mother or my daddy was wearing. I think I gave him some kind of description, like my daddy was wearing a hat and my mother was wearing a dress. Back in those days, most all men wore a hat and the women wore dresses. He said, "Well very good, I'm sure we can find them with that description." So, he held my hand as we walked about the fairgrounds and about all I could see was peoples' butts. Finally, he took his hat off his head, put it on mine and hoisted me up on his shoulders. "There," he said, "now maybe you can see a little better." As we walked about, I would see people smile at the officer and me and some made comments about me being a policeman. All fear was erased from my body, now I was feeling pretty good about things.

The officer stopped and asked me if I liked cotton candy, and I told him that I didn't know. He said, "You've never had cotton candy?"

I replied with a "No." He walked over to a stand where I could see swirling in a big silver pot this stuff that did in fact look like cotton, and mind you I knew what cotton looked like, except it was blue, and I had never seen blue cotton. The policeman told the man that I wanted some cotton candy, so the man takes a stick and begins to stir around in that pot of blue cotton and comes out with a big ball of it wound around that stick. The policeman tried to pay the man for the cotton candy but the man said no charge for our cities' finest. The officer asked me how I liked cotton candy, and I told him that it was good and that I didn't know you could make candy out of cotton.

He said, "Enjoy it, but don't get it on my head."

We searched the crowd for another few minutes when I spotted my mother and the rest of the bunch. I admit that I was happy to see them. I pointed them out to the officer and he walked over to them with me still on his shoulders.

"Hello," he said, "Mr. and Mrs. Winstead?"

My mother looked at me and said, "Yes, and who is that child on your shoulders?" The officer said that I came to him and asked him if he would help find his family because they were lost. He said that sometimes parents get lost and he had to look for them and when we found them he would tell them to keep up from now on so they don't get lost.

He turned it all around so that the blame would not be on me. I'm sure at the time my parents knew that he was trying to make me feel better about the whole thing.

On our way home I heard my dad tell my mother that the police officer sure was nice. Then Daddy asked me what I thought of the officer, I told him that I really liked him and that when I grow up, I want to be a policeman.

...and so, I did. In 1967 I became a policeman, and was in law enforcement for thirty-four years and have no regrets for choosing that field. My only regret is that I never knew his name, and I wish at some time in my life I could have thanked him for that memory that has lasted me my entire life.

For a young boy back then, you were taught to respect the police, and to me he was more than just a policeman...he was a friend, a knight in his dark blue uniform with the pistol and holster, his shiny badge and buttons and a hat that had a badge that made him seem even taller. I must say, he left a lasting impression on a little farm boy that only dreamed about becoming a policeman and wearing that suit of blue armor. I thank you Mr. Policeman, wherever you are.

I, apparently was not the only one in my family attracted to law enforcement. My older brother, Richard, was a police officer in Nashville, N.C. when I joined the force there. Richard and I worked together for about two years and then he went to the Nash County Sheriff's Department, where he later retired.

I later went to the Sharpsburg Police Department and was hired as chief of police. After Sharpsburg, I worked with the Spring Hope Police Department and then to the Enfield Police Department where I retired. I continued to work part-time with the Spring Hope Police Department for a number of years after retirement.

My younger brother, Don, joined the Rocky Mount Police Department and became a detective. I think it was thirteen years he served all together. Don also worked as a motorcycle officer for some time, but I'm not sure how long.

Me, while working with the Spring Hope Police Department.

(Photo Courtesy of the Spring Hope Police Department ©2017)

Richard, while working with the Nashville Police Department.

(Photo Courtesy of the Nashville Police Department ©2017)

My mother, Minnie and brother, Don. Don worked with the Rocky Mount Police Department.

(Photo Courtesy of Winstead Family ©2017)

My First Arrest

My first job as a police officer was in the small town of Nashville, N.C. Back then in the year of 1967, you didn't have to go to L.E.T. (Law Enforcement Training) at a police academy. I went to see the Chief about a job, and he granted me an interview then and there. The first thing he asked me was, "Are you scared?"

I said, "Of what?"

He asked, "Are you afraid of arresting someone, or afraid of getting hurt, shot, or of anything?"

I said, "No, I'm not afraid of doing my job if that is the question."

He said, "Well I think you will be ok, so here is you a pistol, a badge, a black jack, and I'll see if we have a uniform that will fit you. You need to wear some black shoes when you come to work Wednesday at 8:00 A.M." I gathered up my uniform, gun belt with pistol and holster, and six extra bullets.

The next morning the Chief told me that I would ride around with him for the next couple of days so that he could show me the town and where my jurisdiction stopped, and in the meantime, introduce me to the people in the business district downtown

So, for those two days, that was my training, talking with people, getting to know them and them getting to know me.

That was the extent of my training, nothing about what the laws were, nothing on traffic laws, nothing about criminal laws or town ordinances. Nothing about what constituted an arrest, search, or what forms to fill out in the event I made an arrest. In other words, I knew absolutely nothing about the law or how to enforce it. I guess it was left up to me to just use good judgement, or at least my better judgement.

The Chief told me on Wednesday, that I was to come back to work that Friday night, at 11: 00P.M. for the third shift, and that I would be working alone. Now mind you, in that small town when he said alone, he didn't mean in a car alone, he meant that you were the only police officer on duty. So now the whole town was depending on a young, twenty something year old to protect and serve.

There was a place there in town, on the north side, that was called the bottoms. A place where the blacks hung out, drank, danced and played billiards. This place was known as a very rough place for fights, cuttings, shootings and the likes, and until that night I had never even passed by the place. But, my opportunity to see it more closely had come.

The owner of one of the beer joints was trying to close up because he didn't want to be in violation of state, county, and city ordinances of being open while alcoholic beverages were being consumed and that could jeopardize his liquor license and on premises permit. So, he called the dispatch and requested that an officer come and get everyone out so that he could close. Dispatch called me and said, "Nash County to Nashville 21, 10-25 the Canteen and see owner, reference subjects refusing to leave."

I answered back, "10-4 Nash County." All sorts of things went through my head, how should I handle this, and what was going to happen if they refused to leave when I ordered them to leave. Back in those days we didn't have portable radios, so once you left the car, you were on your own.

This being my first call was a little nerve racking, but I was determined that one way or the other, I was going to handle it.

First of all, when I got to the bar, there was a lot of activity outside. People were drinking, cursing and arguing all out in front of the place. I basically had to push my way through the crowd and with some smirks and mumbles from the crowd, I was able to make a path to the front door still intact. I found my way inside where I was met by the owner. He advised me of his situation and requested my assistance in getting the people that were refusing to leave, to go outside.

I went to the very back where the poolroom was located and started herding them to the next room which was the music and dance room. Then with all them headed to the front room which was the bar, I able to get them toward the door in which most left without incident. But, as I was to find out, not all people will appreciate your authority as a police officer, or the fact that I was the only navy bean in a pot of pintos. I guess I stood out like horse in a phone booth.

I noticed one guy about thirty years old, sitting in a booth drinking a beer. Politely, I walked over to the table and told the man he would have to stop drinking and leave the premises because it was already past the drinking hours. He just looked up at me with a snarl on his face and said that he was not going to go anywhere until he finished his beer, and for me to get the hell on somewhere else. Needless to say, that didn't set to well with me so I reached over and grabbed him by his collar and dragged him from the booth. When I pulled him out, he was a bit surprised and ended up on the floor on his knees. He reached into his pocket as if to retrieve something, and not knowing what he might have in his pocket, I reacted by smacking him beside his head with my fist. He rocked over on his side and again fumbled around trying to take something from his pocket. This time I used my blackjack (powered lead incased in leather.) That time was enough to daze him so that I could put him up against the wall and search him and apply the handcuffs. I found out that what he was trying to get out of his pocket was a hawkbill pocket knife. I put the knife in my pocket and while holding to him I shuffled him to the door. When we reached the door, I intended to push the door, which was just a screen door, open with his body. What I didn't know, was that the owner had the door hooked and it would un-hook it as someone would leave. One someone left, that way no one could come back in.

When I shoved him at the door, he went right through the screen head first and flipped over the bread advertising screen guard that was across the door. I didn't know that the door was hooked until all of a sudden, his feet were up in the air. He was handcuffed with his hands behind him, so the first thing to hit the concrete porch outside was his head. I flipped the hook up and walked out to find several people gathered around with puzzled looks on their faces. I never spoke a word, but reached down and pulled him to his feet swinging him around towards the patrol car, and rammed him against a steel post that held the porch up. It honestly sounded like a bell clapper when his head hit the post. Not wanting to show any sign of weakness or pity, I continued on to the patrol car where I inserted the man and left.

The following morning, Thurman Hyde, the Chief of Police came in and asked me how things went. I told him that everything went ok. He then asked in a joking way if I made any arrests.

I said, "Yes I did."

He looked a little like he didn't believe me and said, "You're joking, right?"

I said, "No, there is one in the jail cell that I put there last night.

He asked, "Who is it?" I told him that I didn't know, just some guy that wouldn't leave after closing time at the bar, and so I had to arrest him.

The Chief asked what I charged him with, and I told him that I didn't know what the charges should be. The Chief went back to the jail cell to see who I had arrested and then told me that he thought that maybe the second shift officers had made the arrest. I asked him why he thought the other officers made the arrest, and he said that every time that guy was arrested, it took two officers to bring him in. The Chief advised me further that this particular person was dangerous, and had an extensive record.

I think because of the circumstances that ensued on that first night, the way things looked to the people that witnessed the arrest, may have given reason for the others to follow my instructions the next time I had to go on a call there. Out of all the arrests that I made there, I had only one to resist, and he never did again. No one knows that it was an accident that I threw him through the door, and banged his head on the steel post. I think that they thought, 'That cop don't play!'

Me and my brother, Richard, while we were police officers with the Nashville, N.C. Police Department.

(Photo Courtesy of Winstead Family ©2017)

Just Plain Stubborn

Another time in my early days as a cop, I recollect this particular arrest that surprised the Chief.

Maybe a few months after becoming an officer, I was working the late shift when I happened to pull out on Main Street and saw a jaywalker crossing the street between the traffic lights which were definitely in violation of a city ordinance. I approached the violator and told him to stop, he continued on completely ignoring me. I followed him for some ways trying to get him to stop until finally I had to exit my squad car and actually put my hands on him in order to stop him. I told him to stop being an ass, but in fact, that's exactly what he was, a mule. He was a pretty gentle mule at that. A short rope, about eight feet long was around his neck, so I led him back to my squad car and held the rope out the window so I could lead him around to the police station. When we got to the station, I tied him to a telephone pole beside the station. I didn't know who the owner was, or who to call, so I decided to wait for the chief to come in on the day shift and see what his suggestion would be.

While, on my way back to the station leading the mule from my squad car, a reporter of the local paper was returning from a story he was covering in a neighboring town. When he saw me, leading a mule down main street, he just had to take that picture and of course it ended up in the papers.

Now, getting back to the Chief coming in on day shift…

Just before it was time for shift change, I lead the mule inside the police station and put him in a cell. The Chief arrived and asked me how things went that night. I exclaimed, "Well Chief, everything went pretty smooth except for the one I had to put in jail." The Chief asked me what did I arrest him for, and I told him I got him for jaywalking. The Chief looked a little perplexed, asked me why I arrested someone for a non-arresting offence? I advised the Chief that the arrestee refused to stop when I told him to, and refused to give me his name. I told him that he was very big and my handcuffs would not fit him so I had to put a rope around his neck and tie him in the jail cell. The look on the Chief's face was priceless.

The Chief said, "Are you out of your mind, I hope we don't get sued." Then he said, "Let me go back there and see if it is someone I know."

The Chief walked back to the cell the mule was in, but I stayed in the office. All of a sudden I heard the Chief bellowing out a huge laugh. He came back to the office with a big grin on his face and said, "You got me!" Then he added, "If he makes a mess in there, you know who will clean it up don't you?"

Fortunately, the Chief knew that the mule belonged to a man that ran a saw mill about ten blocks away. I remember the mule got out a couple more times after that and I had to arrest him again.

(Photo courtesy of The Nashville Graphic ©2017)

Author's Extras

Raymond Hugh Winstead and Minnie Lorena Gardner.

(Photo Courtesy of Winstead Family ©2017)

At my mother and father's 50th Anniversary gathering; (left to right) back row: Richard, me, Don, Floyd, Cecil; front row: Terry, Barbara Mother, Daddy and Frances.

(Photo Courtesy of Winstead Family ©2017)

THANKS TO ALL CONTRIBUTORS

I would like to thank everyone that contributed stories, memories and photos, especially my brothers, sisters, nieces and nephews which helped to make this book possible.

Writing this book brought back many memories of my childhood, and I thought it would be fun to go down memory lane and tell of some of the adventures that I experienced growing up, and tell of my father and mothers as well as my siblings.

Jimmy Winstead

Dirt Roads and Bare Toes made possible by:
Written by: Jimmy A. Winstead
Edited by: Tammy Winstead
Graphics Artist & Designer, cover page font design:
Heather A. Johnson

(Photo courtesy of Terry Winstead ©2017)

Please visit JAWinstead.x10host.com or at https://www.facebook.com/JAWinstead to see other books I have written, along with current events and news.

Made in the USA
Las Vegas, NV
25 April 2022